BAMBOO & BUTTERFLIES

FROM REFUGEE TO CITIZEN

by Joan D. Criddle

East/West BRIDGE Publishing House
Dixon, California

Copyright © 1992 by Joan D. Criddle

Published by East/West BRIDGE Publishing House

East/West Bridge ph. 916-678-8454
Publishing House
1375 Estates Drive
Dixon, CA 95620-3236

Publisher's Cataloging in Publication
    (Prepared by Quality Books Inc.)
Criddle, Joan D.
    Bamboo and butterflies: from refugee to
citizen / Joan D. Criddle
    p. cm.
    Includes bibliographical references.

    1. Mam, Teeda Butt. 2. Cambodia-History--1975-
3. Refugees, Political--United States--Biography. 4. Oral
history. I. Title. II. Title: From refugee to citizen.

DS554.83.M36C5 1992   959.604
                         QBI92-34
ISBN 0-9632205-0-0
Library of Congress Catalog Card Number 92-70276

Printed and bound in the United States of America
FIRST EDITION   2nd printing

*To all those
who have ever adjusted
to a new culture,
especially to the newcomers
who have made America their home.
You and your descendents have enriched,
and will enrich, this nation.*

*And to the United States of America,
a haven for my ancestors and other
freedom-seekers like them.*

- Joan D. Criddle

CONTENTS

PREFACE

"Because Vitou doesn't have family, I feel like his mother," I told a television interviewer the day Vitou and Teeda Mam became American citizens on July 24, 1986. He and the extended family have truly become relatives of mine in spirit - perhaps I was Cambodian in a former life or they my Norwegian kin.

In 1980, I helped bring Vitou, Teeda, and some of their relatives to America. I spent the next seven years figuratively walking in their footsteps as I interviewed, researched, and wrote the biography of their experiences as slaves under the Khmer Rouge in Cambodia. A year to the day after their citizenship ceremony, *TO DESTROY YOU IS NO LOSS: The Odyssey of a Cambodian Family*[*] appeared in bookstores. However, by then I knew that the most important half of their story remained to be told. Readers were left with a brief epilogue saying, in essence, that after the family's hellish years under the Khmer Rouge, they lived "happily ever after" in America.[*]

But what is it like to begin from scratch, a refugee in an alien setting? How do newcomers mesh two vastly different cultures? What difficulties do immigrants face when adjusting to a new homeland? What do Americans do that makes the transition easier or more difficult for newcomers? How can immigrants maintain their cultural ties and still function effectively in mainstream America? Can their experiences smooth the path of acculturation for the next wave of newcomers? What can immigrants tell us about this process and about ourselves? Although the first book was published five years ago, it is only now that Teeda's family and I have felt distanced enough from their experiences as newcomers to try to address these questions.

This intimate view of one family's experiences offers insight into what it is like - and has been like - for all newcomers who adjust to an alien culture under difficult circumstances.

---

[*] *TO DESTROY YOU IS NO LOSS: The Odyssey of a Cambodian Family,* by Joan Criddle, paperback edition published by Anchor Books Doubleday, 1989

[*] Just as *Southeast Asia* refers to more nations than Cambodia, Vietnam, and Laos, so too does *America* mean more countries than just the United States of America. This book, however, follows today's common practice in this country of using *Southeast Asia* and *French Indochina* interchangeably, and *America* and the *United States* interchangeably.

I deeply appreciate the family's willingness to share the American half of their incredible odyssey. At times they had to reach back in memory twelve years, to when they were new in America. As in the previous book, they have allowed the reader to see their failings and foibles as well as their triumphs, so that we may better understand the refugee/immigrant experience.

For mainstream Americans, may this book bring deeper appreciation for your own ancestors' adjustment to America.

May it help all of us empathize with each newcomer or minority person who finds life in the dominant culture difficult.

May it also prove useful to educators and others in helping their students and clients find acceptance and success here.

May it help students walk in someone else's shoes, if only for the length of a short story.

And most of all, may it offer courage and encouragement to newcomers. You are not alone. Others have felt the same frustrations, faced the same prejudice, solved the same problems, and dreamed the same dreams. May this family's experiences and the humor with which they *chose to cope* offer you stepping stones as you seek your own version of the American Dream. And may you do so without denying your cultural heritage.

All of us are (or our ancestors were) hyphenated Americans. It requires courage and determination to begin again in a new homeland. It helps to know we are not the first to tread that path, nor will we be the last. Everyone benefits from heroes and role models, especially from our own cultural roots, and except for Native Americans none of our roots go many years deep in American soil.

Whatever our cultural background, we occasionally need to be reminded how much all of us have in common. This book is written to renew our determination that the United States' motto E PLURIBUS UNUM, *Out of Many, One*, does not become an empty slogan. May we, in our diversity, strengthen national unity by working together and by opening the door to others as it was opened (or as we wish it had been opened) to us and our forebears.

I based this collection of stories on my own observations and experiences plus incidents told to me, over the course of more than a decade, by my Cambodian-American friends. From these scraps, I stitched the bits and pieces into vignettes with a theme or message.

The stories offer several views[*] on a few topics that are important to understanding the immigrant experience. Some exemplify typical situations and problems most immigrants face, whatever their background. Other vignettes ring a note of familiarity across cultures and are as true for old-timers as newcomers; they remind us of our commonalty. Several examine social issues such as prejudice, discrimination, family conflict. And a few focus on contrasts between Eastern and Western cultures and religions.

Ideally, family members would tell their own stories in their own words. They did not feel comfortable doing this, not even with my help. Therefore, the vignettes are presented as first person biographies or oral histories - as was done in my first book about this family. Most vignettes were conceived and written by me, but all were read and approved by the person through whose voice the story is told, to be sure that I portrayed their feelings accurately.

Although these friends, in particular, and others offered suggestions and made contributions for which I am grateful, I remain solely responsible for all stories, excepting those with another person's byline. Two incidents were narrated to me almost complete. I present them with minimal editing under the narrator's byline. Occasionally, I focused discussions on a topic and have delivered the edited conversations. In addition, six stories are by people who knew members of this family during their first months of adjustment.

Many people helped in the book's preparation; I wish, especially, to thank Janet Mayhew, Shirley Jones, Audrey Fowler, Mary Lou Willett, Laura M. Criddle, and my husband, Richard.

In 1988, third grader Siobhan joined her class in writing *Thank You* letters after I shared with them the story of their classmate Helena Hong, Teeda's niece. I cherish this student's final sentence, "You digged for my heart and found it." May that be your response as you mine for nuggets of empathy, understanding, and humor in this book about my "relatives."

---

[*] Certain situations have been described by more than one person; therefore, some repetition is unavoidable between vignettes.

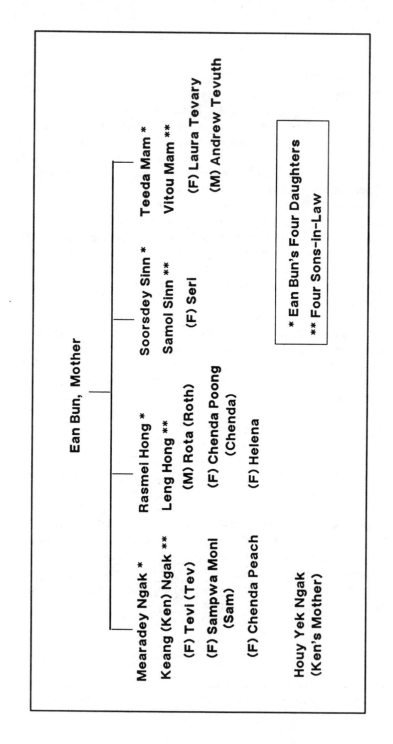

Ean Bun, Mother

Mearadey Ngak *
Keang (Ken) Ngak **
(F) Tevi (Tev)
(F) Sampwa Moni (Sam)
(F) Chenda Peach

Rasmei Hong *
Leng Hong **
(M) Rota (Roth)
(F) Chenda Poong (Chenda)
(F) Helena

Soorsdey Sinn *
Samol Sinn **
(F) Seri

Teeda Mam *
Vitou Mam **
(F) Laura Tevary
(M) Andrew Tevuth

* Ean Bun's Four Daughters
** Four Sons-In-Law

Houy Yek Ngak
(Ken's Mother)

BAMBOO: A Recurring Dream

Flexibility . . .

    Pliability . . .

        Versatility . . .

            Tenacity . . .

All night Teeda tossed and turned. She dreamed of bamboo, shifting, bending bamboo that does not break in the violent storm, because it does not resist the superior force. Cambodians have survived many rulers and invasions because the people learned to bend rather than resist when resistance would only break them. Flexibility and resiliency allowed them to conquer in the end, just as bamboo rights itself when the fury of the storm has passed.

Hundreds of years ago, when Thailand invaded the ancient Khmer Kingdom, it was the impenetrable bamboo jungles around the new capital city that defeated the invading forces - until the Thais devised a clever scheme. While the Khmer Kingdom slept, Thai soldiers threw gold nuggets into the dense bamboo growth that ringed Kompong Luong. Then, the Thais retreated and waited patiently. Discovering gold in their bamboo groves, the Khmer population rushed to clear the bamboo in search of more. By the time they found all the gold, they had torn down their wall of protection. The waiting Thais easily took the city and, of course, reclaimed their precious gold. Cambodians had prized gold more than bamboo, not understanding the value of their bamboo forest to their freedom. This lesson from history has been drilled into Cambodian children for generations, told and retold by village elders. Teeda, as a child, loved to hear her grandmother recount this famous tale.

REINCARNATION
By Joan D. Criddle

Sleek, gentle
Caterpillar
   Brightly bedecked,
   Peacefully grazes on lush foliage
   In a tropic clime;

   Raging typhoons
   Level your world,
   Leaving you wrapped in a cocoon
   Of silence. Dark
Chrysalis
   Drab and still,
   Clings to life,
   Hidden beneath tattered leaves,
   Finding scant refuge
   From the bitter storm,

   At last tossed limp
   On distant shores,
   Gains strength from warming rays,
   Then bursts forth
   Reborn -
   A stunning
Butterfly.

   Slowly, tentatively,
   A new mantle unfurls,
   Revealing vestiges
   Of the Orient - an echoing
   Heritage maintained, but now
   Adapted to another life.
   Exchanging leaf for nectar,
   You thrive once more.

First Family Members Arrive

1 THOSE ARE *MY* NOODLES

Tevi:

Tired and confused, I repeatedly asked myself, "Where am I? Where am I?" Everything seemed alien: unfamiliar surroundings, weird noises, peculiar smells. The people were strangest of all. They looked and acted so odd. Unintelligible words spit from their mouths like rounds from an AK-47.

Trying to gain invisibility by standing stock-still, I hid behind my mother, wary, suspicious, terribly insecure. Except for the flight attendant in Hawaii, no one had actually done anything mean or threatening to us - yet. But we'd been tricked so often in Cambodia after the Khmer Rouge came to power that I took nothing at face value. My response to this foreign situation was skepticism and silence. I'd just watch and wait while I got my bearings.

I was somewhat encouraged by my parents' behavior, especially my father's. He looked apprehensive but not threatened. My mother was obviously nervous but not panicked. They acted pleased to be here, but their occasional reassurances to us children sounded less than assured. Did they really believe we would be safe in this land where the unfamiliar lurked at every turn?

As a girl of nearly twelve, I should have offered comfort to my two younger sisters. Instead, in my attempt to keep a sharp lookout for anything suspicious, I forgot all about them.

We'd left one country in the evening and refueled in the middle of the night on an island my parents called Hawaii. Now it was day again. We, and dozens of other refugees, were

huddled in a huge room in a place they called Travis Air Force
Base.   Sometimes my parents called it Travis, sometimes
California, and sometimes America. I decided they didn't really
know where we were.   I just wanted to go back; the Thai
refugee camp had begun to seem like home. At least the people
there were the right color.

We'd been herded from the airplane and hustled into this big
room by a woman with pale pink skin, bright red lips, and colorless hair, and by a bunch of other men and women who looked
just as ghostly.   Using exaggerated gestures, they repeatedly
shouted "Houston," "Chicago," "New York," and other unfamiliar
words as they grouped people in various parts of the room.

I suspect my eyes were saucer-sized when I spied the first
black person I'd ever seen. It wasn't the huge man's skin color
as much as the kinky hair, the thick lips, and his size that
terrified me.   Many people in Cambodia and Thailand were
almost as dark skinned, but I'd never seen anyone so big and
threatening. He reminded me of the fearsome guardian statues
in Buddhist temples.

Surprisingly, none of the white foreigners seemed to notice
anything out of the ordinary. He walked toward a group of
those colorless people and exchanged a few words in passing.
Soon I noticed several others like him - even some women. I
also saw foreigners who looked almost like us Cambodians.
Americans came multicolored - hair and all!

A woman approached my father. He eagerly held out our
papers and asked, "Parlez-vous francaise?" She shrugged, looked
at the documents and took us to a corner where no other
refugees had been sent. Each time my father approached one of
the busy strangers, they gestured to our corner repeating,
"Stay . . . , stay . . . , stay," firmly but not unkindly. Over the
course of an hour or so the other refugees boarded planes.

Each time a group left, I wanted our family to join them but,
of course, said nothing. Finally, we were the only ones left.

That struck me as ominous. In Cambodia to be singled out by the authorities often meant death. However, my parents did not act overly anxious, just preoccupied. I was hungry but didn't dare mention it or ask why we were still waiting. In my culture children do not question adults' decisions. When parents said, "Sit and wait," we sat and waited.

My hunger pangs brought back the fury I had felt at the rudeness of the flight attendant in Hawaii. I had been jolted from sleep when we landed and the interior lights flashed on. I rose, still groggy, and obediently followed my parents and the other passengers. In the terminal I wanted to curl up and go back to sleep, but we were supposed to eat. The airline people handed each of us a large cup of noodles. I wasn't hungry, so after a few bites I replaced the lid, deciding to save the rest until I really needed it. In Cambodia we'd known starvation, so to me this little stockpile of food represented a lifeline of security.

As we reboarded the plane, an attendant reached for my cup. I clutched it closer. She grabbed more determinedly. "Those are *my* noodles!" I protested in Cambodian. Who did she think she was anyway? In the midst of my struggles, my mother whispered anxiously that I must not anger these people. We needed their help. Reluctantly, I released my hold. The woman casually tossed my container of noodles in a big bag as though it were garbage! I watched in anguish as my precious hoard joined the growing mound of noodles and cups pried from other refugees.

Noting my distress at having the noodles taken, the flight crew tried to mollify me by indicating that more food would be served later. That did not lessen my anger. They'd taken my food. Now I had no reserves. They had no right to take it; they didn't even want it.

They did serve another meal on the plane, but I remained skeptical of their sincerity. I'd learned my lesson. Hunched over the tray, I gobbled every bite before they could change their minds and take it back. By this time I'd entered my shell of wariness.   Outwardly these Americans acted friendly, but exhausted as I was, they wouldn't catch me off guard again.   I decided from that point on to merely observe from the sidelines until I figured out what was really going on.

We'd been waiting at Travis for what seemed hours when at last a Caucasian man and woman entered the room and came toward us waving. The woman smiled as she called my mother by name. At first, her accent kept us from understanding her; besides she addressed my mother by her middle name. The woman obviously knew about family names coming first, but not about a person's first given name being last. (In Cambodia, family names are written first followed by the middle then first given names.)

I wondered suspiciously how she knew us. Her eyes had merely swept the room before she and her husband made a beeline in our direction. Only later did I realize that she came looking for a Cambodian refugee family, and we were the only refugees still in the room.

Her words were as unintelligible to me as all the others, but this time my father responded. I decided they must be speaking French. She was named Charlotte and her husband Robi. They were members of the Lutheran congregation that sponsored us.

In a whisper, my parents expressed relief to each other that someone had come as promised. Either my father and mother had forgotten to tell us kids of that concern or had deliberately kept it from us; perhaps they weren't sure the promise would be kept. Whatever the reason, that was the first I knew why we'd been waiting.

Toting our meager belongings to the sponsors' car, I got my first good look at America. There were automobiles everywhere, some moving but most parked row upon row as far as the eye could see. I tried to take in our surroundings, but Robi's car soon gained speed and everything whizzed by too fast. I kept thinking, "Where am I? What kind of place is this? Look at all these buildings. Look at all these cars. Look at these wide roads. Look at all these different people. Where is everyone going so fast?"

I must have fallen asleep because I don't remember the ride to Davis distinctly. Having seen the tension drain from my mother's face when our sponsors came, I knew it was safe to lower my guard - at least for the time being.

2 LETTING GO

Mearadey:

"Oh, look. They've got corn here too," I cried excitedly to my husband. When we arrived in America with our three little girls, I felt as though I were at sea in a fog. Only occasionally did something familiar surface to which I could cling. Therefore, certain sights and events of those first weeks stand out vividly in my mind.

I first saw the miles and miles of cornfields as Charlotte and Robi Sarlos drove us from the airport to our new home in Davis. In Cambodia corn was grown in small plots. I'd never seen huge cornfields before; nonetheless, they provided my first, tentative lifeline between Cambodia and the alien world I'd entered. I don't know why corn seemed so important at the time. I saw many things I was familiar with, such as cars, buses, airplanes, houses. I guess I just hadn't expected to see corn.

The second sight that struck a strong chord of familiarity was our apartment. But first, our sponsors gave us a short tour of the community I don't remember much of that tour; we suffered from jet lag and nervous system overload. I do remember being driven around the town and the Davis campus of the University of California. Davis seemed small, which surprised me. I thought all American cities would be like New York or Chicago or Los Angeles - places we'd seen in movies and in ads about

America. Davis had no skyscrapers, not even short ones.

As we entered the apartment, I suppose Charlotte was telling us that this was our new home. Gesturing expansively, she and Robi showed us around what we later learned was a very modest apartment. At the time it looked big, clean, and grand. I could hardly contain my excitement; that apartment reminded me of our Western-style home in Cambodia - before the Khmer Rouge drove us into primitive village living.

I knew no English and my French was limited, but I could tell that Charlotte was explaining to Keang (who soon preferred to be called Ken) how to use the appliances, where the food and other household items were kept, which bedroom was for Ken and me and which for our daughters. Clothes hung neatly by size in each closet made it easy to tell who belonged in each bedroom. All those beautiful, clean clothes seemed the height of luxury. Sponsors had furnished our apartment from their own homes and from secondhand stores. They thoughtfully included a black and white television set to provide inexpensive entertainment and to help us learn English.

Charlotte directed our three girls to a box of toys and a little trike for two-year-old Chenda. At this unwanted attention, wide-eyed Chenda Peach whimpered and clung to me while Tevi and Sampwa Moni timidly explored the contents of the box.

We found the refrigerator and cupboards stocked with foods, most of them unfamiliar to me. In the oven, a delicious smelling chicken and a pot of hot rice had been prepared for us by the church women.

Even Cambodian words could not express our gratitude and relief at finding generous strangers willing to help us get established in America.

After Charlotte and Robi left, we were on our own for the rest of the day. For me it passed in a haze of unreality mixed with excitement, fear of the future, relief in the present, and utter exhaustion. Cornfields. An apartment. New friends. I clung to these three precious lifelines I'd discovered on my first day in America.

Within days of our arrival, another sponsor took us to McDonald's to taste "real American food." The hamburgers, French fries, and shakes were good, but the most impressive McDonald products were the beautifully shaped, cleverly hinged, white foam-plastic containers. Although our sponsor seemed embarrassed, I insisted on taking them home.

Why, I thought, would people throw those lovely boxes away? They were valuable. Anyone who had lived under the austerity of the Khmer Rouge could find dozens of uses for them. They could be sewing kits, dishes, jewelry boxes, pots for seedlings, containers to hold the children's treasures. Leftover food could be kept in them. Children could cut them up for their art projects. They would be great for holding paper clips, thumb tacks, stamps. . . .

A day or two after we arrived, Tevi and Sampwa felt safe enough to join the other children at pool-side; I envied children's ability to communicate without language. Even my husband, Ken, seemed to adjust to our new surroundings. For two-year-old Chenda and me it was different. Chenda was born during our years of slavery and reared in poverty with never enough to eat. Her pinched little face viewed the world with wary eyes. She would not let me out of her sight.

I was exhausted physically and emotionally from years of hard labor and the struggle to survive. Coping with a new culture and learning a new language overwhelmed me. I felt handicapped and incapable - a broken reed just when I needed the resiliency of bamboo. The self-confidence I'd had as a wife and mother in prewar Cambodia was gone. A ringing telephone startled me. I refused to answer it. A knock at the door often went unheeded. I feared leaving the apartment; someone might talk to me in English, and I would be unable to answer. If I got lost, I couldn't even ask for directions to get home. So, from behind our curtained windows, Chenda and I looked on, wishing we felt free to venture outside in the hot July sunlight. For a time, however, I could absorb no more new things, pleasant or otherwise.

I remember the first time I heard the voice of water; it terrified me. Two distinct sounds alternated: a slow cha, cha, cha, cha, cha, followed by a rapid hat-t-t-t-t-t, and back to cha, cha, cha in an endlessly repeating pattern. That menacing sound continued for hours, but not always from the same direction. Even today, the fear and anxiety of those first weeks in America returns each time I hear that sound. And what was so menacing? The Rain Bird sprinkler system watering the grass at the apartment complex.

Television became my constant, unthreatening companion during the weeks of adjustment. I couldn't understand the words, but the shows provided diversion and eased the loneliness. One day I watched General Hospital. I didn't know what the actors said, but their actions made the basic plot clear. The next day I recognized the same actors. I decided the show must be a repeat program but watched it anyway. After tuning in for several days I finally realized that the program used the same people, but the story was not the same; it was a continuing story. That intrigued me. I'd never heard of soap operas before.

From television I learned some English, but I also gained impressions about life in America - most weren't reassuring. Fortunately, many of my negative impressions have proved false, but not all. American culture as shown on TV seemed (and still seems) very wicked. Skimpy bathing suits and open displays of affection shocked me. In Cambodia we'd seen Western movies, but even the chaste kisses in those imported films had been edited. At first, my daughters put their hands over their eyes in embarrassment during kissing scenes. Soon though, I noticed the gaps between their fingers widening as curiosity overshadowed embarrassment. Before long, romantic scenes had become so commonplace we paid them no more attention than did our American friends.

School started two months after we came to America. Sponsors had tutored Tevi and Sampwa during the summer so they could fit into a school routine without too much trouble. In September Ken, too, took English classes at an adult school, but I stayed home with Chenda. The two of us were even lonelier with the others gone all day. The world began to close in on me.

Although the thought of braving this new culture frightened me, I knew I must. Otherwise, I would forever be an outsider, trapped by fear and a language barrier. The time had come for Chenda and me to break out of our protective shells. Mustering all my courage, I enrolled her in a cooperative nursery school, at the urgings and with the help of our sponsors, particularly Mary Lowry. Nursery school put Chenda Peach in contact with children her age and me with their mothers.

In addition, I volunteered to work in the library at Valley Oak, my older girls' school. I might not know English, but I could sort and file books by their numbering system. I needed to feel useful, to contribute. I had no money to offer, but I did have time, and that I gave gladly.

Each mother worked at the Davis Parent Nursery School two mornings a week. However, I usually went every day that the library didn't need me. I knew I must be around people who spoke English if I were ever to learn it, and Chenda needed me near. At first she cried a lot but gradually left my side, enticed by the activities and her new friends.

Not knowing a chart had been prepared to show which activity each mother was to supervise on a given day, I wondered how the other mothers always seemed to know exactly where to station themselves. I suppose the teachers explained the system, but I hadn't understood, so I never checked the assignment chart. Instead, I wandered from sandbox to craft area to some other corner where a child needed comfort or someone wanted help with an activity. In their kindness, I guess the mothers and teachers just worked around me, filling in where I should have been, until I caught on. I learned a lot besides English at that school, thanks to empathetic mothers and teachers.

Good experiences at both schools and with our sponsors speeded my adjustment to America. Besides giving me English lessons at the apartment, sponsors included me in their church and community activities and let me run errands with them. Their wholesome lives gave needed balance to my negative TV impressions of Americans.

As my language skills, assurance, and knowledge of the community increased, the trauma of culture shock lessened. Gradually I dared let go of the past, focus on the present, and look forward to the future.

There is a Cambodian saying: *Learn from the past but live in the present.* It took several months, but at last I felt ready to do just that.

3 KEN'S STORY
Narrated by Ken Ngak

<u>With Minimal Editing:</u>

The first thing that shock me after we got out of the airplane and all the other refugee left, we were alone. It was so quiet. I went outside and look around. I felt we had been plop down somewhere alien. I felt we were lost somewhere in the world. It was so quiet; we were accustom to crowds and noise - in the refugee camps, in Bangkok, on the plane, in the airports. Travis Air Force Base so quiet; I felt so lonely, like I was losing something.

Finally, two of our sponsors came for us. When Charlotte ask if I spoke French, I was very happy. I knew we could manage if I could communicate with someone.

In Bangkok they told us the name of our sponsor - the Lutheran Church in Davis, California - and that someone would meet me and my wife and three daughters. There was a map in the Bangkok camp and everybody try to find the state and, with luck, the city they were sponsor to. We try to find out where we were going. We had no personal correspondence with our sponsor. We were process too quick for that. We were in the Bangkok camp only one week.

The reason the American Embassy process everyone so fast then was, at that time, Thai students began demonstrating around the camp. They say they didn't want the refugee in their country. "Send them back. Send them back." They keep saying that. People inside the camp who could understand Thai told us that the students want to send us back to Cambodia. I was so afraid. Thailand got money from the United Nations for the refugee, and the students were demanding more money, or to send us back.

The American Embassy personnel quickly built a fence around the camp so the students can't see in, or us out. They warn us not to go outside the camp because the situation unsafe. The Embassy start processing papers twenty-four hours a day. After seven days, about eight o'clock in the evening, I hear the loud-speaker announce our name that we would take a plane to America the next evening. I was so happy. I couldn't believe it happen so fast.

Before we left, the embassy people let us tour Bangkok one day. Then we went to the airport and left for California. Before we left, we wrote letters to our relatives in France and to a friend at the Thai-Cambodian border. Mearadey also post our sponsor' address on the bulletin board in the processing center in case anyone who knew our family could tell them where we went.

In America, Charlotte and Robi Sarlos take us to the apartment. The first thing Charlotte say was, "This your place. This your home now," she said in French. I couldn't believe it. The room had a carpet; that was a nice thing we never had in Cambodia. There was food, a table with five chairs. Charlotte explain to us how to use the kitchen appliances. The electric stove the only thing we not use before. We didn't know we would be provide with an apartment. We had no idea what would happen to us in America. I ask, "Are you sure this for us?" Charlotte explain, "This your home now. All this food. All the clothes and all the furniture. Everything." Unbelievable.

We got to Davis early afternoon, July 9, 1979. As soon as Charlotte and Robi left and we were alone, then we really start to check everything. We explore. The children were so exciting about all the toys. It was very well organize; they had arrange the clothes according to the age of the people. It seem like they already knew our measurements! It fit our girls perfectly.

In the evening when it start to get dark, we hear the sprinkler noise. We didn't know what it was. I still remember that sound - very scary - and the sound of the toy music box, the jack-in-the-box. We didn't sleep much that night. It was day for us. I stay up all night with excitement.

Early in the morning I walk around the house. I look through the curtains and saw the trees. I thought, "Wow, these trees look like our trees." I saw the street. No one was there. It was early in the morning in the summer time. It very quiet. I began to realize that the movies not depict America accurately. In the movies I saw Los Angeles or San Francisco or New York: big cities, skyscrapers, traffic, lots of people and noise and action. I thought that was America. I keep thinking, "If we are really in America, how come it so quiet? Maybe they trick us; maybe we back in Cambodia instead."

Next day Charlotte take us grocery shopping and show us how to buy food at State Market. That store had the best supply of

Asian food in town. She told me, "You have $20 to buy food for the week." I was concern. I wonder what kind of food we could buy for so little money. Most items were unfamiliar to us. Sometimes I pick up the wrong thing, and Charlotte tell me, "No, you do not want that." Or she say, "That too expensive." I was shy, so I let Mearadey walk with Charlotte to do shopping. She can do better.

At first we sleep most of the time, all day and all night because of exhaustion and jet lag and relief. The next week we do all the physical exams. I didn't start school until September. I didn't work either. We just stay home and mostly sleep.

From the first time we went to the market I start worrying about how we going to live in America. I want to know how could we manage on so little money. I didn't know how long financial help would last. Then what was I suppose to do? Did they intend to feed us for the rest of our lives? No one explain what was expect of us or when.

Then Charlotte start asking me if I plan to go to work very soon, or what else I plan to do. I say, "Yes, I want to work, but right now I don't speak English. I can speak and write French, but not English. Is there some kind of work where they need people who speak French? I can do that." She say, "No, I don't think so. Nobody here needs much of that." Later I realize that even if there was a need for French speakers or translators it between French and English, not French and Cambodian.

"Well, you are going to have to start working soon because the church will run out of funds," she said gently. I learn the total funds for the family is only $1300.

I say, "Well, I am going to have to find some way to get into school first." She say, "Well, you had better think about it." I say, "Okay, I will think about that and let you know."

Few days later a young Cambodian woman, a student from UC Davis came to visit us. I think our sponsor Mary Lowry arrange that. I ask the student lot of questions about how she do when she first got to America. She explain us everything in Cambodian. That make us much more comfortable. She explain to me the first thing I need is to get into school to learn English. I ask her how I could earn a living while I was in school. She explain that since we had three minor children, we eligible to receive some public assistance. She say we should apply. I didn't know what is this "public assistance." I think Mary found out about this and told the student to explain it to us.

We didn't know where these funds came from or how much we could get or for how long. We didn't know there were special funds to help refugees for three years; maybe our sponsors knew. I told Mary what the student say, and she told me she knew about the welfare, but she didn't want us to have to use those funds. I say, "Mary, I want to work. I don't want to stay on welfare, but give me some time. I like to go to school first. It won't be long. I just want to learn some English then I apply for a job." She agree to take us to the welfare office to apply for the assistance.

We felt freer now. We weren't totally dependent on the church. We could decide how to spend our money. I felt so relief because when we went shopping there was nobody behind us. It was a very tight budget.

I took English classes for three months at the Fremont Adult School in Sacramento. I want to stay in school longer, but each time they gave me an achievement test, I alway pass. So they move me up through the classes. The problem was that in writing I could do quite well. I understand, but I couldn't speak. I need more time and practice.

I felt very frustrate, because when I talk in what I thought was English, it seem like they don't understand me! I couldn't understand them either, but when they write, then I can understand. In the highest class, the teacher say, "Well, Mr. Keang, I think you had better get out of here. Leave the place for someone else." I couldn't understand what the man say. A student near me explain it. I say, "Why?" "Because this is too basic for you. You need college level English as a Second Language." I only got to go to English classes for three months.

When the older girls and I began school, Linda Schmidt came to our home sometime. She teach Mearadey some English.

One sponsor saw I had a French-English dictionary, and that I use it often. He say, "Oh, you can read a dictionary and are quick." Seem like he impress. He say, "Well, if you can't go to that English class no more, you need some other school." He mention a business school in Sacramento and ask what I was interest in majoring. My cousin in Los Angeles told me that computers are good field since this is the age of the computer. So I want to go for that.

I apply for financial aid; the school told me about that and help me complete the forms. The tuition was $2400 to complete the program. I got $1700 in financial aid. The remain had to come out of my pocket. I ask the school how I could pay that; I didn't get enough from welfare to cover that. They say, "Don't worry. Start paying when you get a job." I say that fine, and decide to go for it.

They put me in a class of about twenty-five students. Most were girls. I wonder if I was in the right class. It was a keypunch entry level course. We in class six or seven hour a day. I take many computer programing course and related course. The business school is at O Street and 24th. I had very hard time understand the lectures. I bought a lot of books and study COBOL program and several other program, plus keypunch, typing, accounting, math, business.

When all the teacher lecture, I didn't understand anything, first because of the English and second because of the technical language. A Korean student, with a master's degree in political science, sat next to me. We became friends. He couldn't find a job in his field, so he enroll in business school for more training.

He spoke good English. After school we sat in his car, and he explain what the lecture was about. Then I complete the work at home with my dictionaries. Some words I can find, some I can't. They too technical for a general dictionary.

It was very hard, very frustrate. I study really hard for the first three months, and after that I begin to feel comfortable. I start to understand what the teacher say and got use to the books a little more. The hardest was typing. I did very poor. My fingers didn't move right. Everybody but me pass that class. I had to repeat the beginning course. I pass the second time. I can type 45 words per minute.

At the end of the school, I got a diploma. It was very exciting to get a diploma in America. I was so proud of myself. But where to the job? That was the hard part. Mary took me to the *Sacramento Bee* newspaper because she know someone there. She thought my computer work might could be use there; in Cambodia I was a newspaper man. When we got out of the car, I saw people carrying banners in front of the building. I ask Mary, "What are they doing?" She say, "They on strike." I don't know what "on strike" mean. We pass them and go inside. Men working in the computer room were typesetting. The man in charge ask me lot of question about how do I know about the newspaper, and what do I do in Cambodia in my newspaper career.

I explain that at first I work for the Cambodian News Agency, originally as a writer/reporter for two year. After that, I was transfer to the National Radio Broadcasting. I work there three year. In writing room six or seven people working under me. I translate cables from various international news agencies - AP, UPI, the French, and the Russian news agencies, etc. Most cables were in English, except the French agency ones. I use a lot of dictionaries there, too, for translation. I also wrote Cambodian news for the government (only favorable to government). I also wrote more honest editorials for a local newspaper; the editor was a friend.

The man at the *Bee* ask me how I know about the computer, so I explain him about my classes and what we study. He ask if I could write a program. I say, "Yes, a small program. I can write in COBOL." He say, "Good." He let me out and ask Mary for a phone number and to keep in touch, and say he let me know if he might need me. Then we came home, and we never hear anything since.

I went to the employment office in Woodland, to the CETA program, and to others to put my name on their lists. Then I ask Mary to introduce me to a man at the church who was a programmer at UCD. I explain my training and that I need a job. He talk to a woman at computer room who need help.

Each day they went through about ten box of paper, and each box weigh thirty to forty pounds, and only women working there, so they hire me. I haul the paper and did a lot of printouts. For a week they train me, and after that they let me do the job. Now the women could take it easier. I was so happy, because now I could do something to earn a living! I felt good that they trust me and let me do the work by myself.

I punch some keys to enter some commands, but most of the program already done and just runs. I did all kind of jobs. I try to do really well so they would like me. A few months later they trust me to print the payroll checks. That was very exciting because they trust me. At first when I did the checks someone was looking over me, behind me, to see if I was doing okay before they trust me. I was a stranger to them. Then they trust me to do the job without checking.

One time a check was printed wrong - for $70,000! Everybody run to me asking what was wrong. I didn't know. I was very scare. It wasn't my fault. All I did is start the checks through the printer and punch some command keys and the checks start to print. The program was already there. I was so scare at the time. The supervisor said, "You don't have to be scare. It not your fault, it just a keypunch error." I so happy; I had work very hard, try to please everybody.

At first I use a hand truck to bring paper from another building quite a distance away. They saw me doing that one day and decide to give me small truck to haul the paper, instead. I was so happy to drive a truck with my work. I work there four or five months.

I think maybe our sponsors thought I change my mind quickly after they work hard to get me the job at the university. I was lucky to get it. They couldn't understand why I went to San Jose and left that.

While I working at UCD, a long-time family friend who live in Union City learn I was in Davis. We had work together in the National Broadcasting Company in Cambodia. He came to see me in Davis. He ask me how much I got paid at the university. I say, "$5 an hour." "Are you happy?" "Yes, I'm happy. I got a job. I can rely on myself."

Then I ask him what other Cambodians were doing to earn a living in America. He say mostly business. He recommend me several business, mostly doughnut business. He told me a friend of mine, who came to America when I did, live in San Jose, and now he manage a doughnut shop and own a home already. After one year in America and he bought a home? It seem unbelievable. I ask him how he do that. He took me to San Jose to meet my friend.

They ask if I was content to work at UCD at $5 an hour for my whole life. They ask, "How you going to own a home, raise a family, put three kids through college? Can you afford to do that for $5 an hour?" I was impress when I saw my friend own a home just by being a doughnut shop manager for one year. He ask me, "Why don't you come, and I will train you and will help you get a store?"

I didn't give up my job at the university quickly. I got train in doughnut business in my spare time. I want to see how I like it first. I left Davis after dinner every Friday and learn how to cook the doughnuts, every weekend.

EPILOGUE TO KEN'S STORY

In a few months Ken was trained, at no expense to anyone but himself. He then applied for and received a manager's position before quitting UCD. After a short, formal training course, he became a manager at a Winchell's Donut House not far from his friend's shop. So in the spring of 1981, Ken and Mearadey left their three children in the care of the extended family. The two older girls wanted to finish the school year at their elementary school, and Grandma could tend Chenda Peach. Ken and his wife moved to California's Silicon Valley and worked every shift at the doughnut shop. They hired minimal outside help. Friends let them share their cramped quarters; those who worked nights slept in the beds in the daytime, and those who worked days used the beds at night. Conditions were crowded, they worked day and night, but before the summer ended, they'd saved enough to rent a home of their own in one of the less affluent sections of town.

Until this time, Mearadey and her sister Rasmei had relied on their mother, Ean Bun, to watch the two preschoolers and the four older children while the other adults worked or went to school. With Ken and Mearadey in the Bay Area and Rasmei and Leng's family still in Davis, they needed to decide where Grandmother would live, and who would watch the grandchildren in the other city. Rasmei's family resolved the problem by moving to the Bay Area too. They and Grandmother moved in with Ken and Mearadey's family in the rented house.

Ken, Mearadey, and their two older girls kept busy running the Winchell's shop, and within a year had saved enough to buy

a small ice cream parlor in a run-down shopping mall.
Mearadey managed the ice cream shop. The older girls helped
her after school and on weekends. Ken continued to run the
Winchell's store.

Before long they bought their first home - a beautiful, brand
new house in one of the area's desirable subdivisions - at a time
when interest rates were in the mid-teens! To make ownership
possible, the extended family pooled resources for the down-
payment and all moved in. Not long after, they again pooled
resources for a down payment on Leng and Rasmei's new home.
When Teeda and Vitou completed their associate degrees in
Sacramento a year later, they moved in with Ken and Mearadey.
Within a couple of years, the extended family again assisted in
making a down payment so that this young couple, too, could
buy a home of their own.

In short order, Mearadey had transformed the sluggish little
ice cream parlor into a thriving business which she sold at a
handsome profit. She had other plans for her life. Ken left the
doughnut business about the same time. They took more
schooling and worked other jobs before deciding to make a
major career change. This compassionate couple chose to leave
the security of their higher-paying jobs for employment with
Santa Clara County. They wanted to work with immigrants and
refugees. Having surmounted many of the hurdles most
newcomers face, Ken and Mearadey knew they could bring a
special dimension to the work. Grateful for the help they had
received, they wanted to devote their energies to assisting
others as a way to pay back America's investment in helping
them get established in a new homeland.

4 SAMPWA MONI BECOMES SAM

Sam:

I was eight the summer we moved to America. By then I'd learned to fear change; it was usually bad. I decided I'd probably dislike America as much as I'd disliked leaving Phnom Penh years before.

Until I was four, I lived with my parents and older sister, Tevi, in my grandparents' home. My two cousins, Rota and Chenda Poong, and their parents lived there too. We four children had a great time. Never short of playmates or indulgent grandparents, we also had two teenaged aunts who read stories and slipped treats to us. Other relatives lived next door, so we had free run of the neighborhood.

Nothing marred my sense of security until bombs fell on Phnom Penh. Terrified by the explosions and the sound of helicopters flying overhead, I learned fear. Being forced from our home and from the city was a shock, lessened only slightly because all my relatives were with us. Then the Khmer Rouge took my grandfather away.

We were not allowed to go back to Phnom Penh, so my family settled in a farming village. Rota and Chenda Poong's family was forced to settle in another. No longer having them for playmates, I came to depend on Grandmother for companionship as well as solace. The other adults worked away from the village all day every day.

Our home was not nice like the one in Phnom Penh; our hut had one room and palm frond walls. We ate in a communal dining pavilion. The food was watery, not very good, and never enough. When Tevi turned eight she had to live away from home in a children's compound. She became part of the work force too. I seldom saw her. Everyone was always tired and had little time to play with me.

For almost four years conditions steadily worsened. Each year the Khmer Rouge forced people to work harder and eat less.

Neighbors kept disappearing, taken away by the authorities. Then the sound of bombs came again, accompanied by the frightening whir of helicopters. Shortly after that we began our escape from Cambodia. One of my few pleasant memories of the five months it took us to escape was of being with cousins and other relatives again - all but Grandfather. He never returned.

We lived with our relatives in a refugee camp in Thailand for six weeks before landing at Travis Air Force Base in California. I planned to dislike America, especially since our relatives weren't with us. Only my parents, Tevi, and my two-year-old sister, Chenda Peach, came to America with me. I especially missed Grandma and my cousins.

While still at the air force base, I formed my first impressions of our new homeland. They were not positive. I felt threatened by all the fair-haired, blue-eyed, light-skinned people. Some white people even had orange hair. Blacks in the crowd were another surprise; the men's short, wiry, black hair was nothing like ours. At first I thought they wore hats. It alarmed me to find that none of these multi-colored foreigners made sense when they talked.

Little Chenda Peach alternated sleep with crying. My parents were tense; Tevi looked frightened. I took my cues from them and silently eyed my surroundings with suspicion. I didn't know where we were or why we had come, but I didn't like it. I wanted to return to the refugee camp in Thailand.

My attitude toward America changed markedly when our sponsors showed us our new home. It was a real house - well, an apartment, but it looked grand to me - not like the hut we'd been forced to live in when the Khmer Rouge were in charge. It was more like our home in Phnom Penh before the war, not that they looked alike, but both were built in a Western style. From the living room of our apartment I spied kids in the swimming pool. America might be okay after all.

The refrigerator and cupboards were stocked with strange foods. Over the next few days we tried them, liked most, and found some inedible. We didn't like the small cans of pudding, but the fruit wasn't bad. However, we couldn't understand why Americans ate canned fruits and vegetables when their grocery stores had beautiful produce. The food I'll never forget was the can of ham in our refrigerator. Imagine, meat from a can instead of an animal. Tevi and I couldn't get over the color of bananas and oranges either. Those fruits are supposed to be green. Who ever heard of yellow bananas? However, they tasted almost as good as Cambodian bananas, so we decided not to let the funny color keep us from enjoying them.

Our bedrooms were another pleasant surprise. Closets bulged with clothes; for four years I'd seldom had even a second set. And the toys! Even in prewar Cambodia we seldom had store-bought toys except a ball or two. We Cambodian kids made our own toys from what we scavenged. If I wanted to play house, my mother or grandmother had helped me roll a scarf and tie knots in both ends. It made a wonderful baby to cuddle. But in America we had real dolls and even a baby bottle with milk that disappeared! We had trikes and bikes, story books, building blocks, and doll dishes.

Our sponsors felt the need to explain to our parents that the toys were not new. That didn't matter to me. Tevi and I especially loved the jack-in-the-box; Chenda Peach hated it. She liked the music when we turned the handle, but each time the clown popped out, she looked startled, then cried.

And oh, the magic of television. Even a black and white set was a novelty. Tevi and I tried to discover how they got all those little people in the box, but we couldn't. We soon became cartoon addicts. Superman was our favorite. Tevi fell so in love with this cartoon character that when the movie came to Davis a year later, she spent her hard-earned $1.50 and bicycled all the way to town just to see it. I liked Superman too, but not $1.50 worth. The next year when our cousins arrived, their sponsors gave them an old color TV. Tevi and I grew envious; each morning before six o'clock, we dashed to their apartment for the day's first cartoons.

It was a sizzling July when we arrived. I could hardly wait to join the other kids in the pool. What an anatomy lesson I got there! A woman came out of her apartment almost naked. Tevi and I averted our faces. We couldn't imagine any woman walking around like that without embarrassment. What shocked us even more was that no one else even noticed. Not only was she wearing a bikini, it was a loose weave knit. We felt such shame and embarrassment for her that we wanted to say, "Go put some clothes on." Except for bare arms, women in Cambodia showed as little skin as possible; to do otherwise would have been dreadfully sinful. But kids adjust quickly; in almost no time we ceased feeling embarrassed by skimpy swimming suits, our own or anyone else's.

Afternoons that summer found us in the pool with our new-found friends. I guess communication wasn't a significant problem; at least I don't remember feeling frustrated or embarrassed or left out because of it. Between watching cartoons and interacting at the pool and playground, our English developed rapidly. Playing, as we did, with white, black, and Hispanic kids, I soon forgot they'd once seemed strange. They couldn't remember to call me Sampwa so I became Sam. I liked it. And my sister Tevi became Tev; nicknames made us feel accepted.

When we weren't swimming, playing with our toys, passing judgment on new food, or watching television, our favorite pastime was treasure hunting in the dumpsters. At first, Tev and I just tagged along with Tobin and the other kids from the complex, but soon we were as quick as the others to jump in the big blue containers to sort through our neighbors' trash. It was great fun, but our mother thought otherwise. She discouraged garbage collecting and encouraged swimming.

My first summer in California was a turning point in my life. I shed an aversion to change almost as readily as I learned to shed my clothes for a swimming suit.

5 BIKES, VENDORS, AND TOMATOES

Tevi:

I felt rich and proud. I owned a bicycle. It was old, it was a boy's, but I hardly noticed. It was mine. Our sponsors gave the old, black Schwinn to me, and I was quite determined to master riding it my first summer in America.

Under the harsh restrictions of the Khmer Rouge, almost no one had access to, let alone owned, a bicycle in Cambodia. Bikes represented a degree of freedom and a level of wealth that the leaders were determined to stamp out. The tight control exercised over us made a bike almost useless for all but mid-level leaders with special permission to travel between villages. High officials, of course, used cars and trucks. The rest of us were not allowed outside the confines of our village except, under supervision, to work the rice fields or clear jungle.

Before the Khmer Rouge came to power in 1975, bicycles were common. However, bikes were not playthings; they provided transportation for the working men and women in place of cars. Piled high with goods, they substituted for delivery trucks. Men earned a living pedaling trishaws - those three-wheeled bikes that served as inexpensive taxicabs. At rush hour, Phnom Penh streets had resembled the start of a huge bicycle race as riders dodged trucks and cars, each one vying for a spot on the crowded roads.

When I arrived in Davis, California - bicycle capital of America, so they claim - I was not surprised that many adults rode bikes, but I was surprised that most children owned one, sized to fit.

Within days of our arrival, I mastered the art of balancing on two wheels. However, no one told me about traffic laws, or if they did, I hadn't understood. Almost immediately I ran afoul of the law. I presume there had been traffic lights in Cambodia's capital city, but as a little girl, I'd not noticed or had forgotten about traffic signals during the years we lived in primitive villages under Khmer Rouge control.

In innocence and ignorance I ventured from my quiet neighborhood onto a main thoroughfare. I biked along, paying no heed to intersection lights as they changed from red to green and back again. They might have been decorations for all I knew. Therefore, you can imagine my shock when a car, approaching from a side street, struck my back wheel, tumbling me to the asphalt. I sat dazed with skinned knees but otherwise unhurt, except for my sense of pride. It was severely bruised.

How rude! was my first and lasting reaction. There I was, minding my own business, riding near the edge of the road, just as my father advised. And then this car, that seemed to come from nowhere, ran into me. To my utter amazement, the driver, after seeing that I wasn't really hurt, acted upset with me. I felt wronged. After all, his car hit me; I'd done nothing to him. "Look at me," I wanted to shout, "I'm just a little girl, my knees are scraped and I've been needlessly frightened. You should be apologizing, not scolding."

Not knowing I was breaking laws or doing something danger- ous, I'd had no reason to feel guilty or frightened, but when the policeman arrived I *was* scared. The agitated driver, with words and gestures, indicated that the accident was my fault. I didn't understand much English, but there could be no mistaking that I was being accused of wrongdoing. The officer believed him! I was incensed, but didn't dare show it since I lacked the ability to express my indignation in English.

When the officer realized that his lecture to me about red and green lights was to no avail, he took me home. My poor mother must have been in a panic when she opened the door to police authority; in my country we'd learned not to take such things lightly. Neither my mom nor I fully understood the officer's explanations, but we guessed he was trying to tell her to watch me more closely and to teach me about traffic rules.

My second encounter with authorities was equally unpleasant. My parents had a small vegetable garden where we raised food for our needs and for extra income. While my parents worked in the garden, it became my job each Saturday morning to bike to the Farmer's Market in Central Park with a basket of produce. I joined other vendors who lined the sidewalk to sell their wares. Each week I claimed an unused spot, displayed my offerings on the ground, and waited for customers. Soon my bundle of squash and other vegetables had been exchanged for cash, and I peddled home again. Several weeks passed before two people approached and asked to see my permit.

"Permit? What permit? What are you talking about?"

"You need a permit to sell here. Can we see your permit?"

"I don't have one."

"Well then, you can't sell here."

"But what about all these others?"

"They have permits."

I didn't know if I should feel guilty or picked on. Maybe they were prejudiced toward Cambodians, or perhaps permits really were required. How was I to know? All I could do was pack my goods and leave, thus ending my short career as a vendor.

When my parents told some Cambodian acquaintances about the problem I'd had trying to sell produce, they warned us that Americans had lots of strange rules. For instance, people weren't free to chop down nearby trees for firewood, keep chickens or pigs in their back yards, or cultivate unused land. You couldn't even catch fish without buying a license.

Before long, I concluded that everything in this country was already owned by someone, and that Americans had laws that regulated everything else. Each time our family turned around, it seemed, we bumped unpleasantly into another law. The consequences so far had been minimal; we just had to stop the activity when some authority said to do so, but I wondered if the police were keeping a file on us. If so, we might be in real trouble despite our best efforts to be law-abiding.

That is why I didn't dare take the delicious looking tomatoes that littered the road later that summer. I wanted them desperately but didn't know if I could legally pick up tomatoes that fell from the trucks. For all I knew those roadside treats belonged to someone, or perhaps only certain people had permission to collect them. Maybe people needed a license.

During Cambodia's prewar years everyone gathered wild herbs, fruits, and vegetables, or hunted and fished at will, but under the Khmer Rouge taking any food for private use was a major crime - serious enough to result in execution. I didn't know what constituted a major crime in America, so, tempting as those tomatoes were, I dared not risk taking any.

What a shock it had been the first time I saw a truck filled with tomatoes, and there wasn't just one truck. For weeks dozens and dozens drove down the county roads from the farms. I'd never seen so many tomatoes in my life. The mystery of those tomatoes became an obsession. I kept wondering, "Who is going to eat all those tomatoes? Where are those trucks going?" I didn't know about canned tomatoes and was unaware of the Hunt-Wesson cannery in town. In fact, at that time I didn't know how fruits and vegetables got in those cans in the first place, but I just couldn't get the trucks and tons of tempting tomatoes off my mind.

Trucks lost a few tomatoes as they rounded corners or gained speed on the straight stretches of road. Most falling tomatoes squashed on impact or were run over by other vehicles, but a few landed tantalizingly in the weeds. Would anyone return for them? If not, were they free for the taking? I couldn't be sure, especially since I didn't see anyone else picking them up. Ultimately deciding I'd better be safe than sorry, I resisted the urge to take any and finally turned my mind to less dangerous things.

My previous encounters with officials in the few months I'd been in America were enough to keep me from daring to harvest that tempting roadside crop. I had no desire to be confronted by authorities ever again.

6 SEARCHING FOR SISTERS

Mearadey:

I was worried sick about the fate of my mother, my three sisters, and their families and found it hard to concentrate on adjusting to America. I'd not heard from my family since June, when they were taken from the Thai refugee camp and returned, at gun point, to the Cambodian jungles.

Previously, they had escaped to Thailand with us. In the refugee camp we all filled out forms for sponsorship to America, but the papers for my husband and me and our three daughters were processed first. We left for the Bangkok transit center for final processing before being sent to California. We felt nervous about being separated from the rest of our family, but officials promised that the others would follow shortly.

Instead, the political climate changed, and our relatives were among the more than 42,000 refugees ordered back to Cambodia by the Thai government. We learned of this shocking decision just before we left for America. I was stunned.

The media reports of appallingly high death rates among those forced back left me devastated. To be returned to that Cambodian hell after escaping it once was a cruelty I could not understand. Why? Why had they been sent back? Why were promises not kept? Why my loved ones? And why had the forced return been to the rugged, remote mountains of north-western Cambodia where survival seemed almost impossible? Why? My mind was a whirlpool of whys that gave no peace.

I knew that I must come to terms with this tragedy if I were to meet the needs of my husband and children and get on with life in America, but my thoughts kept returning to my family back in Cambodia - or in their graves.

Living in comparative ease while they suffered made me feel guilty. I held little hope for their survival, yet felt unwilling to mourn their deaths. I realized I'd probably never learn what happened to them. Likely they'd died of starvation, stepped on a land mine, or were eaten by jungle creatures. Their bodies might be rotting in Cambodia's western jungle where they would never be found. But maybe, just maybe, they'd survived. The limbo of not knowing their fate seemed even worse than knowing they were dead. At least then their suffering would end, and in a way, so would mine.

Coming from a culture in which personal identity is tied tightly to the extended family, I felt as though the most important part of me had been crudely amputated. I was not whole. Loneliness and helplessness gnawed at my heart. Summer heat radiated off the hot sidewalk outside our California apartment, but I felt a chill no sun could warm. In America my days were full, but I was empty. Trying to fill the void, I began writing letters. Perhaps by establishing ties with surviving relatives who had escaped, I could learn something about my mother and sisters. If nothing else, contacting survivors might reestablish my sense of wholeness as part of an extended family. Letter writing filled many lonely hours and served as the major release for my emotions during our first months in America.

I knew the address of an uncle in France. Each letter I received from his family connected me to others I loved and things familiar. Letters contained news of distant relatives and friends and, occasionally, addresses of those who had escaped and been sponsored to France, Canada, or the United States.

But nothing about my mother, my sisters, or their families.

In Davis we were the only Cambodians, so, aside from my husband and daughters, I had no one to talk to, except superficially. I soon spoke enough English to make my basic needs known but not enough to share what really mattered. My difficulty with the language and Americans' general ignorance of our culture and of our tragic past and present left a gulf in our friendship. Through letters, my depression lifted somewhat because I could express my feelings in my native language to people I knew would understand. It helped.

As my correspondence network expanded, I learned the fate of many relatives and friends. Occasionally, I heard welcome news about a surviving countryman we thought had been killed years before by the Khmer Rouge. More often I learned of yet another who had died in the Cambodian holocaust. Strangely, even that eased my mind. At least their fate was known.

In addition to the handful of relatives who had found refuge in a Western country, a few other relatives still lived in refugee camps in Thailand. I wrote to them as well, but none knew what had happened to the ten, no, eleven people so important to me; my sister Soorsdey's baby would have been born by then.

Most surviving relatives, of course, still lived in villages in war-torn Cambodia. However, no postal service operated there so it was unlikely that any letters would reach them.

I tried another tack. Before leaving Thailand, we'd met a Cambodian woman married to a Thai. They lived in the border city of Aranyaprathet. I wrote to ask if it might be possible to arrange for someone to be sent secretly into Cambodia to search for our relatives and bring them out. She replied that she'd found a man willing to risk the border crossing to look for them in our chaotic, war-ravished country, and, if found, guide them out for only 7000 Thai Baht per person (about $350 each).

The news was both encouraging and devastating. In theory it was possible, but in practice impossible. We didn't have that kind of money, certainly not for eleven people. We received

$500 a month from the fund Congress allotted to refugees for a limited time while we got established. Rent took $250. From the remaining $250 (which worked out to just $50 per person), the five of us had to meet all our other expenses. It would take us years to save the needed $4000; it might as well be four million. Nonetheless, I began saving.

In addition, I wrote to my uncle in France asking if he could loan us the money. Although his family had lived in France since Cambodia fell to the Khmer Rouge in 1975, they were, unfortunately, unable to raise that much money either.

All I could do was write back to the woman in Aranyaprathet and to a few other acquaintances along the Thai-Cambodian border, asking if they would try forwarding my letters with anyone traveling between the two nations, usually smugglers. I enclosed money with each letter to pay the carriers; they knew they would also be paid by the person to whom the letter was addressed. The promise of more money when the carrier got to Khum Speu, our ancestral village, helped insure that he might actually try to locate the addressee. To increase my odds, I sent many such letters.

Each letter contained our address, phone number, and the addresses of every known relative in a Western country. Those addresses were vitally important since they would greatly increase likelihood of sponsorship for my family and speed the process, if they were still alive, and if they ever made it back to Thailand.

Considering the Thai government's mistreatment of them before, Ken didn't believe my sisters and their families would try escape again, but I knew they would. The risks were high; at least half of the refugees who tried died in the attempt. But I knew that as long as my three sisters were alive, they would never give up trying to get out of Cambodia. Nor would my mother. Therefore, neither would I give up trying to help them.

I knew that my letter writing effort was a long shot, but if my mother or any of my sisters or their families survived and ever reached our ancestral village, they desperately needed our address. It would be their passport to freedom once they reached Thailand. They *must* know we were alive, that we had made it. This knowledge would give them added courage in their next escape attempt. If they again reached Thailand without our address, they could easily meet with the same fate they did the first time. But if they could prove to Western authorities that they had family in America, they would face almost automatic approval for refugee sponsorship here.

This letter-writing frenzy helped me through our first summer in Davis. I kept it up when our two older girls and Ken began school in September, and when little Chenda Peach started pre-school a short time later. My mind was never far from concern for my mother and sisters or from trying to think of another way to contact them.

In mid-October, three months after we came to America, the letter I had been praying for, but feared I'd never see, arrived. Postmarked from a Thai prison, the letter from my sister Rasmei told of their second escape from Cambodia and their current imprisonment in Thailand as suspected spies. I felt such relief; to say that a Thai prison is a vile place is an understatement, but at least they'd escaped Cambodia. Surely, that last obstacle could be overcome.

Rasmei's letter said they had been amazed to learn we were in America already. That statement helped me appreciate what a short span of time had actually elapsed. During the months of frantic letter writing, time had dragged for me. It seemed that I'd waited forever for replies to my letters when, in fact, all that I've described took place between June 10, 1979, when they were forced back to Cambodia, and the middle of October, when Rasmei's letter came.

From her letter, I learned that most of my relatives never returned to Khum Speu. They'd survived the minefields, the starvation, the disease, and made it out of the mountainous jungle to a road that led to the center of Cambodia, then retraced our original escape route to a Cambodian city near the border. Against all odds, Rasmei's husband, Leng, received a copy of my letter from a smuggler who found him lying deathly ill on a mountain trail not far from Thailand.

The family had already laid escape plans; my letter merely added some assurance that they might actually be successful this time. Soorsdey was seven months pregnant when the family had been forcibly returned to Cambodia. When they reached the crossroads in the center of the country a month later, she knew she would only slow down their attempt to escape and decrease the likelihood of their success. So, reluctantly, she and her husband, Samol, returned to Khum Speu to be with his family when the baby was born. My plucky mother, though ill, and my two other sisters and their families headed west.

Those in the Thai prison with Rasmei were Leng and their three children, my mother, my youngest sister Teeda and her husband, Vitou. Rasmei wrote that before leaving Cambodia, they made many copies of the addresses and other information I supplied. They sent their letters with Cambodians headed for the interior. We could only pray that one of the letters would actually reach Samol and Soorsdey in Khum Speu.

Rasmei next wrote from Buriram, a refugee camp in northeast Thailand. They'd been in prison only fifteen days before being transferred there. My addresses, names, and phone numbers had been the key to their prison release. After checking the information, the authorities conceded that they were indeed refugees not spies. However, they had to remain in Buriram until sponsors could be found.

From our limited income, we'd already sent $100 to the prison so they could buy medicine and a change of clothes. Only a former refugee can know how important a few dollars are in the desperate conditions of a refugee camp or a Thai prison. Unfortunately, the money apparently arrived at the prison after my family left; some official probably pocketed it - at least, my sisters never got it. Fortunately, my relatives in France had sent money and other items which did reach them.

The minute we got Rasmei's letter, Ken asked the Lutheran congregation if they would also sponsor our relatives or help us find someone who could. We needed our family near us, not in a Thai prison or even in another part of America. Within days, five Davis families had agreed to help.

Once I knew my relatives were safe and all eight of them would be sponsored to Davis, my spirits rose. I wished Samol and Soorsdey and their baby could join us as well, but at least their probable whereabouts, Khum Speu, was known. Life in Cambodia was still risky but not as desperate as when we had made our escape.

One morning, about a month after I got Rasmei's first letter from the prison, I got a puzzling phone call. The woman, phoning from New York, identified herself as a social worker who had just returned from work in a refugee camp in Thailand. She had a message for me from my sister. I struggled to understand her; as yet my English was very poor.

"Your sister asked me to let you know that she and her family have escaped and are in the Aranyaprathet refugee camp."

"Yes," I said, "I know they escaped, but they are in Buriram, not Aranya. I just got a letter from them. We have already started the paperwork for them to come to America."

"No," she repeated, "they are in Aranya. I just talked to Samol and Soorsdey before I left yesterday."

That's how I learned they were safe too! I could hardly contain my excitement and gratitude. The social worker gave me an address for Soorsdey. I wrote immediately. I also wrote to Buriram camp to let my mother and other sisters know the whereabouts of Soorsdey, Samol, and their baby daughter, Seri. (Her name means freedom.) Although both groups were only a few dozen miles apart, they'd had no knowledge of the other's successful escape until I wrote to them.

Being a literate family proved to be a vital asset during these escapes, an asset most Cambodians lacked. If I'd not been able to send letters or they to read them and forward my addresses to others, it is unlikely our story would have had such a happy ending, with us all safely in the West. And during the months of waiting, the ability to write to each other was a great comfort to all of us.

I could hardly wait for Soorsdey's letter with its details of their escape. When it finally came, we discovered that the circumstances had been almost as miraculous as Leng's was in getting my letter. Incredibly, within days of Teeda and Rasmei sending copies of it to Khum Speu with several travelers, Samol and Soorsdey received one. They made their escape in record time. Three of my cousins who had not dared join us in our first escape came with them. Knowing we had actually arrived safely in America gave them the needed courage to try.

I began rounding up sponsors for Soorsdey and Samol. Through our friend Bonnie Smith this, too, was done in record time, but not fast enough. Samol and Soorsdey, fearing a repeat of their first experience in Thailand, wanted sponsors immediately. I was crushed to learn they had accepted sponsorship to Canada. I wrote to convince them to wait.

The next week they called from the transit camp in Bangkok. Ken pleaded with them. "Why don't you just wait there? Tell the Canadian Embassy that you have changed your mind. We have sponsors and have begun the paperwork. It is only a matter of time." Ken thought they were convinced, but two days later Samol called again to say they couldn't wait. They were not willing to take any chances by remaining in Thailand longer.

Though bitterly disappointed, I understood their fear and sense of urgency. Their situation was almost a repeat of what we had faced in the Thai refugee camp. We had been working on securing sponsorship through social workers there. At the same time our relatives in France were trying to get papers

cleared so they could sponsor us. By the time they called with
everything in order, we turned them down because by then we
had sponsors in America and had made up our minds that it
offered the best opportunities for us in the long run. Had the
French sponsorship come sooner, however, we'd have jumped at
the chance to join our uncle's family there. Initially, it would
have been much easier had we gone to France. We already
knew the language, some of us had been there before, and, most
of all, our uncle's family and the established Cambodian
community in France would have helped us make the transition.
But, difficult as it has been, we've never regretted the choice we
made to settle in America.

Adjusting to a new culture, learning a new language, and
pulling ourselves from poverty to a middle class standard of
living has not been easy, but it has been worth the effort. We
are lucky to be in America, and we love it.

Historically, Cambodians have held a bias that favors France
because of our long ties with that nation. Cambodia was a
former protectorate, and many of our brightest students studied
in Paris. For more than a century, France was our point of
reference, our window on the West.

In 1987, eight years after our arrival in America, we were able
to afford a trip to France to visit our relatives. At that time, the
advantages of living in America became even more evident to us.
The cost of living is much higher in France. In 1987 the sales
tax was 17%, gas was four times as high as in America, and food
cost much more than it did in California.

We also found that opportunities for higher education are
more limited in France. It is much harder to get into their
universities because there aren't enough. Most people cannot
expect to get a college education. Students who fail to pass the
entrance exam and still want to try for an advanced degree have
only one avenue. They can repeat the last year of high school
and study to pass the exam year after year until they are finally

accepted or give up. In America, students have other options. They can go to a community college, a trade school, or another school depending on their abilities. They can even work for a few years and go back to school full time or part time at a later date. This is not the norm in most other countries.

Comparing our lives to our relatives' lives in France, we realized how fortunate we are to have accepted sponsorship here. The jobs we hold allow us to own homes in nice subdivisions, buy cars, live comfortably, travel abroad occasionally, and give our children university educations. The only Cambodians we saw in France who enjoyed a similar lifestyle were medical doctors, engineers, or those with other advanced degrees in fields that paid top salaries.

Not only have we been privileged to see our relatives in Europe, we've also visited Soorsdey and Samol in Vancouver. They are doing well also. Since coming to America, each reunion with members of our extended family has been memorable, but the reunion I will never forget was the first. It took place at the Sacramento airport in March of 1980, when my mother and Teeda and Vitou entered the crowded lobby. With Sacramento's Channel 3 television cameras rolling, my youngest sister flew into my arms with my mother close behind.

I was unprepared for TV reporter Alice Scott's question. "How do you feel?" she asked, as she thrust the microphone toward me. In my confusion and my joy, English abandoned me. All I could think to say was, "Very s-cited!"

7   THREE SCHOOL SYSTEMS

Tevi:

Education of females in Cambodian was not a common practice, but then, I didn't live in a typical household. By Cambodian standards, Grandfather was a liberal, modern-thinking man. He had no sons, so perhaps that's why he'd seen diligently to the education of his four daughters. He was just as concerned about the education of his granddaughters, and I was the oldest.

I began school in a private kindergarten in Phnom Penh. A year later, my parents transferred me to a private French school. Dressed in my new white shirt and blue skirt uniform, I brought a gift, as expected, to my new teacher of French. Eager to speak a second language, I asked her that first morning to tell me the French word for *earring*. Looking embarrassed, this Cambodian woman admitted she didn't know. A little later in the day, I asked how to say *bucket* in French. She seemed to mentally search for the word then snapped, "That isn't in today's lesson." When my parents came to pick me up, the teacher met them at the door and said I didn't belong there - one day and I'd flunked out! My parents put me back in a Cambodian language school.

Every school in my country followed the French system of exams. All across Cambodia students took tests every six months or so, then advanced to the next level or remained behind depending on their test scores. We learned by rote, with little access to textbooks. Being a quick learner, I advanced both times I was tested, but many students were required to repeat a level or two before moving on, so children of various ages attended the same class.

In addition to the exams, we had to take our first-grade portfolios home periodically to show our parents. My grandfather, as patriarch of our extended family, always reviewed my school work. Usually I showed it to him eagerly, but one time I'd been lazy in two assignments because I didn't like them. The teacher had written a big bold zero on a couple of papers. Although I'd earned top grades on all the other papers, I was ashamed to show my beloved grandfather that folder.

It never occurred to me to hide the poor grades or lie to my grandfather, so I stood silently before him, eyes downcast, and awaited his wrath. Slowly and with dignity, he seated himself, opened the folder and murmured as he leafed through the first good papers, "Uh ha.... Uh ha.... Uh ha...," then, "... *Umm*." I waited without breathing, but he merely paused momentarily then continued leafing. "Uh ha.... Uh ha.... *Umm*. Uh ha.... Uh ha.... Uh ha."

Carefully he closed the folder, rose slowly from his chair, took a ruler from his desk and said sternly, "Give me your hands." I extended them palms up. He rapped them twice, once for each zero. It didn't really hurt, but I felt the reprimand keenly. Then without smiling, Grandfather put his hand in his pocket and withdrew some money. "Here is a coin for each perfect mark," he said, thus dismissing me before turning back to his work.

Grateful that my punishment had not been worse, I vowed silently to never again deserve his disapproval or a hand slap. My grandfather had known how to scold without crushing me; I loved him even more deeply for that wisdom. I ran from the room to show everyone the money; we children seldom had any. Even though my grandfather was quite rich, he didn't believe in spoiling his children.

Within the year the war, which had raged in the countryside for five years, engulfed Phnom Penh, and the schools were closed. A few months later the war ended with the government's defeat. The Khmer Rouge forced everyone from the city. Before we reached our ancestral village, they arrested my grandfather. Of course, that's not what the Khmer Rouge called it at the time. I never saw Grandfather again.

In the village where we settled, our extended family was among those despised as *new people*. We had to be careful not to draw attention to ourselves by doing anything wrong or we, too, would suffer the fate of my grandfather.

About a year after my parents became forced laborers, I turned eight, and the village leaders sent me to live in the girls' section of the compound reserved for children aged eight to twelve. The leaders hoped to make of us a new breed of loyal, young citizens reared on Khmer Rouge ideals. They expected us to renounce family ties, denounce our parents, and shift our loyalty to *Angka* - the leadership.

They called it a school compound, but it was unlike any school I'd known before. Our day began before dawn. We spent the first couple of hours tending the compound's garden plot. Each morning I carried buckets of water from the big pond in our compound to the section of garden I'd been assigned to tend. My eight-year-old legs often buckled under the weight of the containers of water suspended from my shoulder board. Repeatedly I returned to the pond for more water to pour on my thirsty plants.

School proper began around 8 a.m. and lasted about three hours. We recited the times tables, nothing more, nothing less - no history, reading, writing, or other kinds of math. Day after day, year after year, that is all I learned. We had no books. We had no desks, no paper, no pencils. As in Phnom Penh, we learned by rote, this time sitting on the ground in rows. The teacher merely strolled down each row, paused before a student and said, "four times six" or some other combination of numbers. If the child did not answer correctly and quickly, the student automatically raised her hands for the anticipated switching. Over and over, day after day, the teacher drilled us on the multiplication tables. The boys did the same in their section of the compound. No application was ever made of the times tables. No explanation was given as to what the numbers meant. We just spewed forth the memorized answer when the teacher paused in front of us.

The only other topic was *citizenship* - propaganda sessions. The teacher and village leaders often harangued us at length about the need to report our families, and anyone else, for wrong doing or wrong thinking. Other days they admonished us to be diligent workers, to be the eyes and ears of Angka, and to sacrifice our lives if necessary for the good of the new nation that the Khmer Rouge envisioned. They used slogans such as *To keep you is no benefit; to destroy you is no loss* to intimidate us and quoted other slogans meant to urge us on to greater patriotism or to remind us of our insignificance compared to a grain of rice or a water buffalo.

We ate twice a day. School ended about 11 a.m., after which we ate our first meal of the day. After eating in the communal dining pavilion, we were usually unsupervised and free to entertain ourselves until the evening meal and our nightly duties. Considered the most trustworthy members of this new society, we were assigned to guard the vegetable plots at night to be sure no one stole food.

Most often we slept the sultry afternoons away, but sometimes kids swam in the pond, played tag, or caught tiny fish, shrimp, and large crickets. We threaded the wriggling creatures on willows and roasted them whole over little bonfires. Unlike other villagers, children seldom received punishment for eating these extra snacks. I especially liked roasted crickets; they smelled delicious and had a pleasant, crunchy texture.

Occasionally, I slipped from the compound in the afternoon to visit my parents' hut. Like the other adults, they worked in the fields all day, but my grandmother and two younger sisters were home. From Grandmother I heard the family news and passed on roasted crickets, a handful of rice I'd stolen, or any information I'd learned since last we talked.

Children in the school compound enjoyed a little more free-dom and a few extra privileges, but in general our lot was as hard as that of other villagers. We worked hard. We had no privacy. We owned nothing, not even a change of clothes.

We slept in barracks, one for girls and one for boys. Two

platforms made of rough-hewn boards ran the length of each thatched building, with barely room for a narrow aisle down the middle. These platforms were our beds. We had no blankets or pillows. There was no shelf for personal belongings; but then, we had none. We slept and bathed in the clothes we wore. In cold weather we slept huddled together for warmth, a dozen or more girls to a platform. Our all-purpose scarf served as a belt, a head covering, a pillow or blanket. We also used it to secure bags of rice on our back when we had to carry them. When our outfits could be patched no longer, the Angka issued us another pair of black baggy pants and a loose-fitting, long-sleeved, black blouse.

My first village teacher probably saved my life on one occasion, but I didn't know it at the time and considered his punishment of me harsh and cruel. One day, shortly after moving to the children's compound, I found five or six vegetables accidently dropped, or deliberately hidden, near a little-used trail. Instead of taking the vegetables to the leaders as required, I wanted to give them to my family. They had even less access to extra food than I did.

My teacher caught me with the forbidden vegetables and whipped me himself, rather than sending me to the authorities as required. He said, "What you did is very bad, but because your father was once my teacher in this village before we came to power, I have decided not to turn you over to the Angka. Because I respect your father, I have spared you."

Looking back, I realize the whipping had been necessary and kind; under the Khmer Rouge any disobedience could bring death. I'd committed one of the most serious crimes against their system - stealing food - and had been spared. I'd learned a valuable lesson without it costing my life. Had my teacher been less harsh, I might not have taken the need for obedience as seriously. A more diligent Communist would have reported me.

Just before the harvests, children acted as living scarecrows to

save the crops from predation by birds and monkeys. One
afternoon, during my second year in the school compound, I was
assigned to protect a patch of rice in a jungle clearing. I'd never
been there before. Surprised to find rice in that remote spot, I
was even more surprised to find it not yet ripe. Perhaps it was
planted late, I thought. But why?

Near the middle of the field stood a dead tree. Intending to
climb it and shoo birds and beasts from there, I picked my way
through the ripening rice stalks. An unpleasant smell I couldn't
identify and a spongy feel to the ground near the tree puzzled
me. I noticed that rice didn't grow well in that large, slightly
sunken area. Then from my perch in the tree I discovered
pieces of clothing sticking out of the ground and swarms of
iridescent flies working the depressed area. Perplexed why those
flies, that fed on dead animals, would be in a rice paddy, I
suddenly recalled rumors of people disappearing. A shudder ran
through me; I didn't want to know more. Deliberately, I shut
out further thoughts about the buzzing flies, the bad smell, the
scraps of cloth, and concentrated instead on shooing birds.

My third year in the school compound was traumatic. My
teacher committed suicide after learning he'd fallen from favor
with the leaders and was slated for the death trucks. As he lay
dying from the poison he drank, he told his students that he'd
been too much of a moderate at a time when the leadership
feared that faction. He warned us to obey the new teacher in all
things, at least outwardly, if we hoped to be spared during the
purges.

A few days later, while most girls dozed, our new teacher left
his nearby hut with two Khmer Rouge leaders and approached
our barracks. He tapped a girl near me on the shoulder, smiled,
and motioned silently for her to join them. Wondering what
privilege she might get that was denied the rest of us, I quietly
slipped from the platform and followed at a distance.

This young girl - a model to be emulated, we were constantly told - really believed the propaganda about denouncing parents and giving total loyalty to Angka. For instance, just a few days earlier, she hadn't even asked to go along when her parents and younger siblings were told they were being relocated to a better village.

My teacher and the other men chatted amiably as they took this nine-year-old into the jungle. There they ordered her to dig a shallow pit - just her size. When I realized it would be her grave, I retreated. I didn't want to see more. Apparently, she should have been "relocated" with the rest of her family, but because she lived in the children's compound, the leaders had momentarily forgotten about her connection to them.   How ironic, I thought; she had shown her allegiance to Angka by rejecting her family, yet the leaders apparently didn't really believe their own propaganda.   They didn't trust that she had changed.

By the summer of 1978, our third year under the Khmer Rouge, a new analogy became part of the propaganda sessions. To justify the higher rate of "relocations" and the increasingly open killings of entire families, we were told, "It is necessary to destroy an entire tree rather than to try cutting out a diseased branch. The disease has likely spread to the rest of the tree as well and could even infect other trees."

In America I learned a quote from the Bible, ". . . and the sins of the parents shall be visited upon the heads of their children." Whenever I hear that scripture, I am reminded of the girl from our compound - and the fate of thousands like her who died for their parents' *sins.*

About an hour after they took the young girl into the jungle, my teacher returned to his hut, bidding a cheerful goodbye to his comrades at the compound gate, as though nothing out of the ordinary had occurred. Their callous behavior shocked me.

Under the Khmer Rouge, besides learning my times tables, I learned to be watchful, silent, and suspicious of overt friendliness, especially by those in authority.

I encountered a vastly different school system when I was eleven and we escaped from Cambodia. Other than the two years of schooling in Phnom Penh before the war, I'd never been in a real classroom, certainly not one run in the easy-going American fashion. I began school at Valley Oak Elementary in east Davis two months after I arrived in America.

The principal assigned me to Karmin McCrory's combination class of fourth and fifth graders - two years behind my age level. For the first time I felt glad to be small for my age and hoped my classmates wouldn't discover that I was too old to be in their class.

I approached school as I'd learned to approach all new things - with dread. Wary and watchful, I wondered if the teacher's friendliness was genuine or just a cover for a hidden agenda. Was it really safe to speak openly in the classroom? Did Ms. McCrory really expect a thoughtful, honest answer when she asked questions, or was there a *correct* answer she expected me to parrot back? Where was the standard disciplinary ruler or switch? I didn't see children being punished in the classroom; did it take place elsewhere?

In time my skepticism vanished, and I found myself opening totally to this new experience, soaking up knowledge like a sponge. For too many years independent thinking had been forbidden; expressing an original idea could cost a life. Now teachers seemed eager to help me learn and encouraged my curiosity.

Within a couple of years I skipped a grade. So despite the handicap of starting school in America as an eleven-year-old with a first grade education, I graduated from high school only one year behind my age group and entered college on an academic scholarship.

8 TEVI
By Karmin McCrory

She came carrying nothing more than a piece of paper with her name on it. I falsely assumed she was the child of a foreign graduate student, since Valley Oak Elementary School in east Davis has been the home school for children of graduate students who live on the University of California, Davis campus. Upon arrival in the United States these foreign children usually enter our school with little or no English.

In previous years, however, most of the children had been in the lower grades, so I was both elated and a bit overwhelmed when a tiny Asian girl appeared in my fourth/fifth grade combination class that first day of school.

I felt pleased to have the opportunity to learn about the culture of another country through this student, and I was ready to set the wheels in motion to teach our culture to her in any way I could. However, this seemed an almost insurmountable job with the curriculum of two grades to teach and a child who didn't speak the same language as I. How could I communicate with her?

The administration assured me that the best thing was for her to sit in class and absorb as much as possible. The philosophy that total immersion in a language is the best way to learn seemed true for Tevi. With the assistance of the English-as-a-Second-Language Aide and Tevi's attendance in my classroom, it was not long before she could communicate with everyone.

It was in Jan Brady's ESL class that she was first able to tell us that the scar on her wrist was from falling as her family fled through the forest in the night to escape from Cambodia. That was our first insight into her life before coming to America. I can still see her sitting there at the table among the other students, with her sparkling eyes and big smile, eager to learn but not ready to trust enough to share more of her past with us.

The following year, Tevi transferred to West Davis

Intermediate School when her family moved across town. That move left me believing our paths would not cross again, and that I probably would not learn more of her life story.

It was almost a year later when I realized what impact that first year at school had had on Tevi. While attending a meeting at WDI, I opened a student desk to borrow a pencil. To my surprise, it was Tevi's desk; therefore, leaving a note of greeting seemed appropriate. The following afternoon at the dismissal of school, Tevi set off alone for a trek across town just to see me, in response to my note. Since she hadn't notified anyone of her intended visit, she arrived after I had gone home. This left two very disappointed people, especially since we haven't met since.

Now that the story of Cambodia and its refugees is more widely known, my admiration for Tevi and her family is even greater. I will always ask myself, would I have been able to do more for her that first year if I had better understood her background?

9   MINUTES AND SECONDS COUNT

Teeda:

Following rigid schedules proved to be one of the hardest yet most important adjustments our family had to make when we settled in America. We could not have guessed beforehand how much stock people here put on a precise hour, let alone fractions thereof.

When a sponsor said they would meet us at 9:15 in the morning, they didn't mean 9 o'clock or 9:30. When a television program was slated to start at 7:30 p.m., or a teacher scheduled a parent-teacher conference for 4:45 in the afternoon, it meant just that. When someone said they would pick us up for church between 9:35 and 9:40 Sunday morning, they expected us to be waiting on the curb.

At the school door, time was counted in seconds - or so it seemed. The second before the bell rang you were early; the second after, you were tardy and must face the consequences.

Having a specific time to be somewhere is alien to our Cambodian souls. In our culture time is relative, so it took us many months to realize that it rankled Americans when we arrived earlier or later than the time stated for the appointment or activity, or if we weren't ready when our sponsors arrived to take us somewhere. In fact, we often started getting ready when they came for us; we didn't know they might consider this rude. Or, we arrived at our host's home an hour before the dinner party - we just wanted to visit with them before the crowd arrived or see if we could help with last minute preparations.

I suspect people attributed our apparent inability to keep to a schedule to our being mentally slow or perhaps to our language limitations. Sometimes, of course, we did fail to understand their rapid-fire English, but our continued disregard for time was not a lack of understanding what they said. It was a lack of believing that they meant it.

When my nieces Sam and Tevi started elementary school in America, their family didn't have an alarm clock. They hadn't needed one before. As a result, the girls were often late or extra early for class. They went when they got ready. Fortunately for them, their teachers were quite forgiving of their erratic arrivals, attributing it, perhaps, to the *unreliability* of foreigners. When the girls finally realized they were expected to be on time, they listened diligently to the radio each morning for the time to be announced so they'd know when to leave for school. However, if they failed to hear the announcement, they just kept listening. Half an hour later it was again announced, but by then they were late. I'm sure their teachers never knew how hard my nieces tried. It was not evidenced by the results.

By the time my husband and I arrived in California, eight

months later, we thought my sister, brother-in-law, and nieces were exaggerating when they gave examples of the stress Americans put on being on time. How could we believe their stories, especially when they almost rolled on the floor with laughter while they told us these fantastic tales?

Why, for instance, was it vitally important to rush to the doctor's office at precisely 11:30 a.m. only to wait for an hour or more to see the doctor? Yet, if my sister was to be believed, if you showed up a half hour late, the receptionist might say you'd missed your appointment and you would have to reschedule it for another day. This rigidity in rescheduling seemed especially true when dealing with the welfare department. People there apparently took delight in inconveniencing recipients.

And were we to believe that a person could possibly be expected to know how long it would take to drive across town? You might have to stop for a red light; there might even be a traffic jam or an accident. We chuckled at the thought of our sponsors driving around the block more than once if they'd miscalculated by a minute or two and arrived early. They must do something like that, we thought, else how could they always arrive at the exact time they said they would?

One of our sponsors fascinated me because whenever we planned to do something together she whipped out a little black book from her purse. Besides what looked to me like an already full schedule, Kathryn's appointment book overflowed with additional notes on bits and pieces of paper. It bulged at the spine, held closed with rubber bands. Before agreeing to an activity, she studied the dog-eared pages as one might consult tea leaves. Then she wrote down the exact time in her book and took care to repeat it to me before we parted. Sometimes she even wrote the schedule on a piece of paper and handed it to me. Eventually, I took the hint and made a point to be ready *on time*, even if it meant I'd been sitting in anticipation for half an hour before she arrived.

Another sponsor, Joan, seemed almost as addicted to time management, but her drug of choice was a desk calendar by the telephone. Since Vitou and I lived with her family for a few months, I could peek at all the things she wrote down.

It soon became apparent that by working to a schedule, these women accomplished a great deal. I even began to envy them, wishing I had more than a couple of places to be in a day so I'd have an excuse to carry a Daily Planner. It seemed very professional to check your schedule before making commitments.

Three years after arriving in America, I finished formal education and began working in my profession. I soon purchased a little black planner of my own and could hardly wait for an excuse to see Joan and Kathryn. When we met - by appointment, of course - I whipped out my Daily Planner and stated self-consciously, but proudly, "Now I'm a real American too!"

10 MY FIRST HALLOWEEN

Tevi:

I'd been in America three months and at Valley Oak Elementary just one when I noted an air of anticipation at school. Orange and black streamers, bats, cats, and women in black clothes and pointed hats decorated our classroom. My English speaking ability was still marginal, but a month into the school routine, I had finally felt safe enough to relax my vigilance. Still, I didn't like the classroom's changed look. The witches' black clothes reminded me of the horrors of the Khmer Rouge regime and the black outfits we had to wear then.

I didn't like the cutouts of ghosts any better. Many Cambodians, especially older village women, believe in ghosts. Some ghosts are friendly, some mischievous, others wicked. Most of us from the cities didn't believe they existed but just in case, we let them be. We didn't know how to appease the local spirits - if they really existed. We'd been told that it takes time and skill to figure out what offends local spirits, so we took the precaution of not venturing into unfamiliar places, such as jungles, where they might lurk.

In contrast to my dislike of the classroom's ghosts and black witches, I had no objection to the jack-o-lanterns, but carving faces on squash seemed a strange, extravagant custom. Obviously Americans didn't want for food when pumpkins could be squandered for mere decoration.

As October advanced, the kids at school began asking what I was going to be for Halloween. "Be? Be what?" I wanted to ask but didn't. What did they mean *BE?* I was me. How could I be anything or anyone else? Before long, however, I caught on that everyone planned to wear a costume when the great day came. They were going to pretend to be a ghost, witch, princess, pirate, superman. . . . I knew all about pretending; I'd pretended ignorance, compliance, enthusiasm, obedience, and dozens of other things under the Khmer Rouge just to stay alive. But I'd had little experience in pretending simply for fun.

We had no money for costumes. What could I do? I didn't dare ask my parents to splurge on something as unnecessary as a costume, but I wanted desperately to fit in, to be a *real* American kid. Then a classmate said she was going to be a "beautiful lady" by wearing a woman's fancy dress, draping a scarf around her shoulders, donning high heels and putting on lipstick. Relieved, I realized I could create a similar costume from among the clothes given to my family.

Now I, too, looked forward to this American holiday, one that most kids said was their favorite. I would be given lots of candy, so they said, just by dressing up, knocking on doors, and repeating magical words that sounded like "TRICKER TREE."

A party at the Lutheran church was my first Halloween event. To our delight, some sponsors bought new costumes for Sam and me and even little Chenda. These wonderful outfits seemed much better than having to wear old clothes that dwarfed us.

Proudly, I put on my doctor outfit. Sam wore a princess costume, crown and all. Chenda Peach was a clown. She cried all evening and clung to my parents.

Costumed children ran wild with excitement. Sam and I joined the fun. We enjoyed good things to eat and played great games. Then our friends urged us to go through the spook alley. I didn't know what it was, but since all the others were going, I agreed to join them.

I couldn't figure out what they were so excited about. The kids said we would crawl through this long line of boxes and come out the other end. Big deal. It seemed kind of dumb to crawl through a dark box, but they kept saying, "Come, come, come," so I followed them.

It was pitch black in the tunnel, and the ceiling hung too low for us to stand upright. Crawling along, we had to put our hands into what I later learned were typical spook alley items: Jell-O, spaghetti. . . . Since I didn't know it was supposed to be blood, brains and so on, I couldn't understand the point, and I certainly didn't feel scared. I didn't know I was supposed to be. I just kept crawling through the fake spider webs, the booby traps, and the dry ice smoke.

At one point I lost track of the other kids. Suddenly a lighted face lurched at me. I freaked out and with a reflex action swung with all my might. To this day I don't know which church member I hit in the stomach with that belly-whopper punch, but I heard the air escape his startled face.

In terror I fled for my life. In my mind I was back in a Cambodian jungle being chased by ghosts, demons, or the Khmer Rouge. For weeks after, I felt betrayed by friends and adults who should have been ashamed to play such a cruel joke on an unsuspecting refugee child. But, of course, those secure Americans had no understanding of the depth of real terror I'd so recently fled.

11   A BIRTHDAY PARTY

Sam:

Lauralyn was my first friend at school - for a long time, my only friend. We couldn't understand each other's language, but we had a great time together anyway. We were both second graders; although I was a couple of years older than the other kids, I'd never been to school before. One day we'd almost finished making a castle in the sandbox when Lauralyn left for a few minutes.

While she was gone, a boy about my size, but several years younger, eyed me for some time then deliberately kicked at our beautiful sand castle. I didn't understand his words, but the ugliness in his voice as he shouted at me left no doubt about his meaning. He didn't like Cambodians, at least not me.

Ordinarily, I backed away from unpleasant situations and aggressive people, but our sand castle seemed worth defending. I didn't want Lauralyn to think I'd destroyed it in her absence. In my distress, I defended that pile of sand as tenaciously as a tiger might her cubs. I sprang at the kid, hitting, kicking, pulling his hair, and grabbing his shirt.

Lauralyn and a Yard Duty person had dashed over by the time I realized the boy was crying and trying to get away. Again, I didn't understand the words, but the Yard Duty's message came across clearly as she lectured me. She wrote my name down. I knew I was in big trouble. I felt guilty for hurting the little boy and frustrated because I didn't have enough English to explain my aggressive response. I don't recall now if the school took further action against me, but the thing I feared most didn't happen. The fight didn't lessen Lauralyn's friendship.

Not long after the sandbox tussle, she made me feel special by inviting me to her birthday party, a slumber party. I'd never been to either before and didn't know what to expect, but I'd been included with the other girls and that was enough for me. Since birthdays aren't celebrated in Cambodia, I didn't know to take a present. Fortunately, that didn't seem to matter to Lauralyn, nor did my lack of English keep me from having a great time playing the games. The cake, the candles, the traditional games, and singing "Happy Birthday" were all new and exciting experiences. In addition, Lauralyn had a doll house and lots of dolls. They were fantastic.

The slumber part of the party was fun also, but it puzzled me. I couldn't understand why rich American children would choose to sleep outside on the ground instead of in their wonderful soft beds. I'd slept on the ground or the floor for four years, but not by choice.

The part about that party I remember best was breakfast. I woke to the smell of cooking. It seemed an odd time of day for a hot meal, but I didn't want to keep anyone waiting, so I hurried into the bathroom, brushed my teeth, combed my hair, and dressed before going to breakfast. To my surprise, the other girls, still in pajamas and hair uncombed, were already eating. They'd not even brushed their teeth. Yuk! I thought, again surprised at how Americans did things.

I slipped into an empty chair and accepted the heaping plate that Lauralyn's mother put in front of me. I'd never seen food like this before, so I eyed the other girls and copied their actions. I drowned the pancakes in maple syrup and took a bite. Hot, soggy, sweet - double yuk! I wanted to spit it out but dutifully swallowed. I tried my luck with the link sausages. Twice as bad. I wondered how the girls could gobble down sweet and salty food at the same meal. Why, since Americans were rich, did they eat such awful stuff? I forced myself to take each bite and washed it down with orange juice, which tasted sour, or with milk, which had no taste at all.

I moved across town the next year and lost track of Lauralyn, but I'll never forget her friendship at a time I needed it most, nor will I forget her party and my first introduction to American breakfasts. It is surprising I ever agreed to try pancakes and sausages again, but that menu, so distasteful to me then, has since become a favorite.

12 COPING SKILLS

Tevi:

Most children simply avoided interacting with me when I began school in America. I was *different* and spoke badly broken English. Several made an effort at friendliness but gave up when communication broke down.

My inability to express myself effectively vexed me far more than it did my hoped-for friends. They could always find someone else to play with, but I was left alone. More in thoughtlessness than by design my classmates drew a circle that excluded me just when I most needed to be included. I wanted so much to be accepted, to be one of the gang.

Only a few kids were openly hostile, but they apparently took delight in picking on the "refugee kid," and this made my life miserable. Fortunately, a hero arrived on the scene in the guise of Toby, a boy from our apartment complex who went to the same school. I will always be grateful for Toby's kindness in the face of adversity. He usually rode a bicycle, but because I walked to school, Toby walked beside me and pushed his bike.

On our way to and from Valley Oak Elementary, other kids hurried by laughing, pointing, and calling out, "Lovebirds. Lovebirds." I didn't know what a lovebird was or why they called us birds. Embarrassed, Toby did his best to explain they meant we liked each other, that I was his girlfriend.

When I realized they were teasing us, I appreciated Toby's kindness even more. His mother must have taught him well, I thought, because despite his obvious discomfort at the taunting, he continued to escort me for several weeks until I could fend for myself. "Don't worry," he said with bravado, "just ignore them and they'll soon get tired of it." Stoically he put up with the barbs, proving the genuineness of his compassion for a skinny little girl who needed to lean on his optimism until her own natural cockiness and self-assurance returned.

Later that year my self-confidence suffered another blow. One girl in our class of fourth and fifth graders, seemed twice as mature as the rest of us. Everyone liked her. I wished desperately to look and act as sophisticated and be as popular. Physically she had become a young woman and dressed the part: stylish clothes, shoes with a bit of a heel, and a touch of makeup. If I were like her, I reasoned, then I'd be popular too. So one morning, I woke extra early, dressed up fancy and tried to fix my hair. The night before I'd looked through the box of donated clothes in my mother's closet and claimed a pair of silver high heels that I decided would do nicely.

Walking to school, I discovered that the shoes didn't fit as well as I'd thought. They clacked noisily on the cement with each step I took, and my ankles wobbled disgustingly. Even curling my toes didn't stop the noise. At the intersection my ankle gave way and I fell. Picking myself up from the gutter with all the dignity I could still muster, I continued the final block to school, glad I'd left home early. Not many kids were on the streets yet, so none of them saw me fall or heard my noisy shoes.

As I walked, I became aware that people driving by were looking me over. I wasn't sure if their stares were in ridicule or admiration. I chose to believe the latter but felt my confidence eroding. My teacher was the only one in the classroom when I entered. Stopping her work, she put an arm around my shoulder and suggested kindly, "I don't think you want to come to school dressed like that."

Embarrassment spread across my face as I realized she was right. It was not the right time or place to dress as I had, and she wanted to spare me the ridicule of classmates. Feeling like a fool, I hurried home to change. "How could you be so dumb?" I berated myself all the way home and back again.

I grew up a lot that day, but not in the way I'd imagined. I began so full of hope, thinking that everyone would like me, that they'd treat me like they did the other girl. What an idiot I'd been, I told myself, but where had I gone wrong? In time it dawned on me that I couldn't succeed by copying someone else. I had to be me. Fourth grade wasn't the time or the place to pretend to be grown up when I wasn't.

In the weeks that followed, I studied the young woman more closely and discovered something I hadn't noticed earlier. There was a self-assurance, poise, and genuineness about her, just as there had been with Toby. Her attitude and bearing, more than the clothes she wore, set her apart. An inner sense of self was reflected in her clothes, not created by them. She simply *was* more mature than the rest of us.

It took a couple of years before I hit my stride in school. By then I was attending West Davis Intermediate. I had no trouble communicating in English, my grades were good, and I enjoyed a wide variety of friends. However, I'd not yet learned to deal effectively with the bullies who continued to find me an easy target. One in particular kept picking on me. Although we were both sixth graders, he was twice my size. Avoiding him hadn't worked, being nice to him hadn't worked, and ignoring his obnoxious behavior only made it worse. At my wit's end, I didn't know what else to try.

One day in the lunch room he started in again. I guess I'd had enough. To my surprise and almost without thinking, I scooped a spoonful of mashed potatoes, aimed it in his direction, and pulled back on the spoon with my other hand. Bull's eye! That glob of potatoes landed with a splat on his nose and slid down his face. After the initial shock, he started to rise. I thought he would kill me. Instead, the kids started to laugh and his friends told him to cool it. He never bothered me again.

13   A TRIP TO OAKLAND

By accident or by providence, a new world opened for me on October 20, 1979, the day my husband went to a wedding in Oakland with friends. En route, they listened to a radio report about the continuing plight of Southeast Asian refugees fleeing strife-ridden homelands by the thousands.

Their hearts went out to the desperate people, but as with past disasters around the world - both natural and man-made they felt helpless. How could a few friends, half a world away, make a dent in the enormity of the problem in Southeast Asia?

This day, however, they did not absolve themselves of responsibility.   They felt compelled to act.   Before the ride ended, they'd concluded that although they and their spouses could not help everyone, we certainly could help someone; therefore, we must.   They reasoned that together, we could make a real difference in the life of at least one or two people by volunteering to sponsor them to America.   But we knew neither how to arrange a sponsorship nor what it required of us. A few days later, one of our group told a friend of our interest and asked how her church had become sponsors of the Ngaks, a family of five Cambodian refugees.

Our inquiry was a godsend, we were told.   Her Lutheran congregation had recently learned that eight members of the Ngaks' extended family had reached a Thai refugee camp and desperately needed sponsorship. Mearadey, Ken, and their three girls had asked the congregation to be sponsors for her mother, two married sisters, their husbands and three children.

The congregation was torn.   They felt unable to support eight more people, but how could they tell Mearadey that they would not help reunite this family?   They knew something of the anguish she suffered as she worried about the fate of her relatives.   When Mearadey learned they'd been forced back to Cambodia, after reaching the supposed safety of Thailand, she almost lost hope of ever seeing them again.   Several months later, the Ngaks learned that, miraculously, their relatives were alive, had escaped the hellish conditions a second time, and were, for the moment, safe.

Our group was asked if we would sponsor all eight relatives. We felt overwhelmed; our proposed sponsorship of one or two had just multiplied dramatically, but we jumped at the opportunity to reunite this extended family. The congregation agreed to help us arrange sponsorship through Lutheran Immigration and Refugee Services.*

On October 28, eight days after the Oakland trip, the five couples in our group met with Mearadey, Ken, and a Lutheran representative. With relief we learned that their refugee organization would handle all paperwork and arrange air transportation to California from Thailand.* We were glad to learn that we had a few months to get everything ready before the refugees arrived.

We also learned that our government provided limited funds for three years* to help Southeast Asian refugees relocate and become self-supporting. The government - acknowledging partial responsibility for events that led to the need to flee Cambodia, Vietnam, and Laos - tried to meet some of our nation's promises and obligations to our Southeast Asian allies by offering this aid.

For our group's part, sponsorship would mean meeting the refugees at the airport and helping them settle in America. This help included short-term arrangements for housing, food, and clothing, plus assistance in finding work or otherwise meeting

---

* For the address of this and several other organizations that work with refugees, see Appendix I.

* After finding jobs in America, refugees are expected to repay air fare and related expenses so funds are available to others with similar needs. At the rate of about $20 a month, Mearadey's family, as well as her relatives, ultimately reimbursed the relief organization's revolving fund.

* Government assistance for Southeast Asian refugees was soon reduced from three years to eighteen months and then to just twelve. With few exceptions, political refugee status for Southeast Asians, and this funding, has now ended.

their needs until the government's refugee aid program took effect; we learned that this might take two to three months.

Some refugees came with marketable skills; they bypassed government aid entirely. Others needed social service benefits for several months, but all able-bodied adult refugees were expected to be self-supporting by the end of three years when they no longer qualified for refugee funds. *

We were relieved to know that sponsors of these political refugees were not asked to make a legally binding commitment or to assume total financial responsibility for them. Instead, relief organizations expected sponsors to give short-term aid and be an ongoing source of information and friendship while the newcomers adjusted. Any further involvement was up to individual sponsors.

What we learned that night greatly eased our minds. Now we could concentrate on the job at hand: find a place for the refugees to stay, decide how much financial help we could provide, and prepare the community for their arrival.

The five sponsoring families agreed to carry primary responsibility, but decided to recruit friends and the community at large. Of course, we hoped for donations of food, clothing, furniture, and even money from outside our little group, but more importantly, we sought the community's emotional support. We wanted the refugee family to find a welcoming attitude in our town and school system. Involvement of townspeople seemed the best way to forestall prejudice that arises from ignorance. We hoped to increase understanding and empathy toward these Southeast Asian refugees whose culture and history Americans know so little about. They had faced enough trauma for several lifetimes. We wanted to avoid more when possible.

To facilitate community involvement and make donations tax deductible, we ultimately incorporated as a non-profit

---

* For instance, as young adults with no dependents, Mearadey's sister Teeda and Teeda's husband qualified for only $373 per month. They received funds for twenty-one months.

organization. Before the eight refugees arrived, we began a series of fund raisers. Pictures and stories in the Davis Enterprise and The Daily Democrat newspapers told about Mearadey's relatives and requested donated items for two households. The community responded enthusiastically to those appeals and to our soup suppers, pot luck dinners, garage sales, and calls for donations. One sponsor's garage soon filled with a baby crib, chests of drawers, tables, sofas, chairs, and television sets. In addition, we collected ample bedding, towels, pillows, kitchen items, clothing, and food. What the families would not need to set up housekeeping, we sold at the next garage sale. With donated funds, we rented two apartments near Mearadey's family.

Five months after our group's trip to the Oakland wedding, the first of Mearadey's relatives arrived - her mother Ean Bun, her sister Teeda, and Teeda's husband Vitou. Mearadey's sister Rasmei, Rasmei's husband Leng, and their three children arrived later that week.

Within days of the family's arrival, two sponsors, Dr. Peter Kenner and Dr. Ernest Westover, began repairing their teeth. These dentists generously donated countless hours to this effort; the family had been without dental care for almost five years during their years of slavery and escape.

The Westovers, Kenners, Fowlers, Gardners, my family, and many others in the community invited our Cambodian friends to dinners and included them in activities. In fact, when Mearadey's relatives arrived, both our group and the Lutheran congregation informally co-sponsored all thirteen members of this extended family. We tutored them in English and math. When public transport proved inadequate, we took them shopping, to the doctor, to welfare and immigration offices, and helped them get drivers' licenses and other necessary documents.

Deep friendships developed as we got to know each of them personally and witnessed their determination to succeed. We came to admire the bright intellects and ready wits of this outstanding family. Therefore, it distressed us greatly to discover that all too often a double standard applied in government offices; helpfulness varied depending on the presence or absence of a sponsor. We saw that this family and other minority people faced endless roadblocks and hassles when they approached these agencies alone. Often it took several trips before the needed document or other help became available. If we were along, however, smiles greeted them, and the process moved quickly and efficiently. When we waited unobserved in the background while the refugee approached the desk, the same sullen "can't be done" attitude prevailed. Fortunately, our friends met with a better reception in most other settings. Bonds of love, friendship, and increased understanding were forged as the community united to ease the transition to America for this remarkable family.

As sponsors, we stand in awe of their courage, their fortitude, and their ability to learn a new language, take on a new culture, and make a satisfying place for themselves in America. They exemplify the immigrants' energy, determination, and lifeblood that America has always depended on.

What began for our group as a vague desire to relieve suffering and to help those less fortunate soon became something quite different. Our smugness at being the givers and they the receivers ended when we met. *We* are the ones whose lives have changed for the better by our interaction with people from another culture and a family of this caliber. From them we learned never again to take for granted our American freedoms, our physical safety, our abundance, or life itself. Our understanding of words such as adversity, fortitude, perseverance, gratitude, and courage have greatly expanded, our eyes opened, and our hearts enlarged.

Was it an accident or providence that Mearadey's relatives crossed from Cambodia into Thailand, needing sponsorship at the same time that, half a world away on a drive to a wedding in Oakland, some very self-satisfied Americans were prompted to become involved?

PART TWO: 1980 - 1981
Other Family Members Arrive

14 THAT'S WHAT I WANT TO BE
Teeda:
We were scared - no, terrified. It was March 1980, the start
of a new life for us. Entering this land of opportunity as young
adults with less than ninth grade educations, my husband and I
felt deep concern, especially about earning a living.

In 1979, Vitou and I fled Cambodia, then waited in Thai
refugee camps for more than five months before sponsorship was
arranged and our papers cleared for emigration.   Finally, the
impossible was realized; we landed in America.

Disembarking from the Pan Am flight from Bangkok, we
nervously entered the terminal at San Francisco International
Airport with my bewildered mother in tow. Despite jet lag, the
three of us wandered around the building, absorbing sights,
smells, and sounds of America while we waited for our
continuing flight to Sacramento. Vitou spied mechanics working
on a United Airlines plane. He watched for some time, then
turned to me and said, "That's what I want to be."

Coming to America seemed such a remote possibility while we
were in the refugee camps that we'd made no concrete plans for
the future. Along with others, we fantasized about life in our
new homeland, but it was little more than daydreaming. We
couldn't believe we'd ever leave the camps.

The Khmer Rouge had robbed us of the years in which Vitou
and I should have gained the basic skills needed to function successfully as adults in the modern world. Instead, we spent our
teen years in back-breaking labor and in trying to survive one
more day by outwitting our captors. Thinking about a future

had seemed pointless when each day might be our last.

Then in January 1979, when Vietnam broke the Khmer Rouge stranglehold over Cambodia, all our attention shifted to escape attempts and the struggle to find food.   Fourteen months after we began our escape, we were finally entering America. For five terror-filled years the future had seemed a void. We now faced that future and felt ill equipped.

Vitou was twenty-one years old when we arrived in California; I was nineteen. We had limited schooling, and our English was almost nonexistent. We had escaped with little more than the tattered clothes on our backs, almost no financial resources, few physical or emotional reserves, and limited knowledge of how to succeed in America. Our one real asset was determination. At times even that faltered.

Neither of us had ever held a paying job. Our years of hard labor in the jungles and rice paddies had not equipped us with job skills needed in this technologically advanced nation. We felt overwhelmed. Where to start? How to proceed? I wasn't sure we had the energy to even try. Yet here was Vitou fantasizing about a career; we'd be lucky to get stoop labor.

My sister Mearadey's family and our sponsors met the plane when we landed in Sacramento.   They settled us into an apartment in Davis next door to Mearadey's family. Within days, the sponsors had taken care of our most pressing medical and dental problems.   Then, with Mearadey and her husband attempting to be our interpreters, those five American families sat down with us to discuss our long term goals.*

Vitou and I had aspirations and dreams, but we also understood the difficulty of our situation as unskilled refugees. We hated to settle for a lifetime of labor at minimum wage, but we

---

* We grasped only dimly what our sponsors told us that evening. Real understanding came much slower, but for the sake of this narrative, the process has been condensed. Other vignettes describe in more detail the long process of acculturation and our gradual understanding of the opportunities presented to us that night.

were afraid to voice what we really desired, even to ourselves, let alone to our sponsors.   The idea of expecting anything but menial work seemed wishful at best and childish in the face of stark reality.

Our sponsors explained that Congress had allotted funds to help Southeast Asian refugees get established in America. Acknowledging that the refugees' plight was due in part to U.S. policy in Vietnam, and the resulting war that engulfed Cambodia and Laos, Congress had granted asylum to some refugees and made resettlement funds available for a maximum of three years.

Three years is not long to learn another language, adjust to a new culture, acquire marketable job skills, find employment, and become self-supporting.   Nonetheless, we felt embarrassed to accept handouts for even that long from a nation that had already granted us freedom and safety.   Besides, we had our pride; formerly we'd been a self-sufficient, middle-class Cambodian family.

Unwilling to have our hopes raised prematurely, Vitou and I countered our sponsors' enticing suggestions for future employment with our own practical arguments.   We restated what they already knew: we were unfamiliar with American customs; we couldn't speak the language; our education was about junior high school level.   Five years had passed since we'd last been in school.   We lacked funds, and we hated to accept welfare. . . .

Finally one of the sponsors said, "Forget about money, language limitations and all that.   Tell us what you would like to be if those weren't issues.   Tell us what you planned to be had war never come to Cambodia.   Then let's see how much of that dream is still feasible."

Timidly I admitted that before the war, I had always planned to go to college and perhaps even try for a master's or a doctorate.   Few Cambodians had attained these levels of education and certainly not many women, but my father had encouraged my aspirations when he was still alive.

With hesitation, Vitou then shared his dream with our sponsors.   Fascinated by machines since childhood, he'd always wanted to be a mechanic or perhaps even earn an engineering degree. He wanted to repair or perhaps design cars and airplanes.

There. It was out. We waited for our unrealistic hopes to be dashed. Instead, a long, serious discussion began about options, only part of which we understood. One sponsor explained that we must live frugally now and postpone many of our other wants while getting an education and training, or we would spend the rest of our lives on the lower rungs of the job market. The sponsors helped us see temporary government aid as a helping hand not a handout. That made accepting it easier.

Although we failed to grasp the details and only dimly saw the future they projected for us, we trusted our sponsors. Besides, agreeing seemed the polite thing to do. As our English and knowledge about America improved, we eventually understood what they had tried to tell us that night and in succeeding discussions.

We agreed to accept the government's aid. One sponsor pointed out that by using the financial assistance to gain job skills, our future earnings could be much higher, and the taxes* we paid would compensate the government many times over for its investment in us.

Our sponsors were willing to help finance further schooling after the government assistance ended, but we declined this kind offer. Not only were we unwilling to accept more of their money, it seemed unrealistic to try for our highest aspirations. That required too many years of schooling. Basically, we were five or six years behind American students our age.

We knew it would take hard work to master English and gain adequate training before the refugee funds ended in three years, but we were determined to accomplish as much as possible. One thing we'd learned under the Khmer Rouge was how to

---

* Not only was the word *taxes* foreign to us, the concept was even more alien; we certainly didn't understand its significance that night. More than two years passed before someone thought to explain that taxes were something we should have been paying.

work long, tedious hours at mind-numbing tasks - with nothing to show for it except the privilege of living one more day. In contrast, effort expended in America benefited us directly. We discovered that hard work and long hours are closely linked with success here, and we were determined to succeed. To counter discouragement, Vitou and I realized we must keep our eyes focused on our goals, not on the effort needed to get there.

Although we had only partial understanding of where we were headed, the future looked brighter after that evening's discussion. Our sponsors not only gave us hope, we knew they would be there to answer questions, offer advice, and walk us through the maze of American laws and opportunities.

From then on, I could truly say, as I often have since, "In America I never felt poor even when we had nothing. Here we had freedom and opportunity. We could become whatever we were willing to work for." Here we could control our own destiny more than was possible in most countries. Those who have never been enslaved can never fully appreciate what rare gifts freedom and opportunity are. Being poor is merely an inconvenience when you know it need be only temporary.

Each day, Vitou and I rode the bus from Davis to Sacramento to attend a continuation high school. Two months later, when Fremont School closed for the summer, we augmented our government aid with minimum wage jobs. In addition, I took summer school classes in Davis, and Vitou in Woodland. Our sponsors and others tutored us so we could pass high school equivalency tests.

In the fall, I returned to the Fremont adult school. Vitou attended night school and worked days. A year later, having completed our equivalency exams, we were ready for the next phase of our expanding dreams. We enrolled in Sacramento City College.

Most majors listed in the junior college catalog baffled me. I had no idea what they involved, but several majors tempted me. However, we deliberately limited our choices. Knowing we would always be somewhat disadvantaged when competing for jobs with native speakers, we looked for career training that could be completed in a couple of years, wouldn't require extensive English, yet paid well. A counselor helped me settle on data processing. Vitou eagerly grabbed the opportunity to earn a degree in aeronautical mechanics. We felt as if we were living a fairy tale; eighteen months in America and we'd risen from third-world slaves to American college students.

Our well-laid plans for associate degrees came crashing down before we were half way to our goal. Vitou and I had completed only one semester and were mid-way through the second when the letter came. Instead of the anticipated monthly check, the letter said that Congress had revised the rules governing refugee assistance. The three years that refugees had been given to become self-supporting had just been reduced to eighteen months. And since we had received aid for twenty months, not only had the checks ended, we must refund the money for those last two months!

Devastated, we could hardly think. We had come to expect such treatment from the Khmer Rouge, as time after time they had tricked us into a false sense of security, but we'd never expected it of the U.S. government. How could we meet our immediate expenses? What would we live on? Where would we ever find the funds to repay two months' overpayment? Coming as it did without warning, the letter caught us with no contingency plan.

Obviously, we could not both remain in school. For one or both of us that semester's tuition and our investment in textbooks had been wasted. In the careers we had selected, one and a half semesters of a four semester program trained us for nothing. Had we known at the start that assistance would end in eighteen months, we would have laid less ambitious plans. Discouragement enveloped us. Two years in America and we were almost back to square one - and in debt besides.

Unwilling to burden our sponsors and too embarrassed to tell anyone but family about our problem, we worked frantically to regain our footing and salvage what we could of our toppled dreams. Decisions had to be made and carried out immediately. We decided I must quit school, live with my sisters' families in the Bay Area, and work for my brother-in-law at the Winchell's Donut House he managed. With my earnings, I hoped to begin repaying the welfare office and, with luck, keep Vitou in school.

Trying to sound casual, I told our sponsors I'd decided to drop school and move in with relatives, and that Vitou would stay to continue his studies. They were dumbfounded. Why? Didn't I like college? Was I failing my courses? Were Vitou and I having marital problems? Why not at least finish the school year since only six weeks remained in the semester? How could they help? Our sponsors' sincere concern and desire to help touched us deeply. Of course my feeble explanations made no sense to them; I must have appeared ungrateful and irresponsible. Rather than let them think that I finally showed them the letter.

Our sponsors were incensed. They could not believe their government would offer financial assistance, then withdraw it callously without warning. They felt it must be illegal for the government to do so, especially the part about demanding back payment. They immediately checked the original rules regulating aid and found that refugees must be given at least thirty days notice of any change. There had obviously been a breach of contract, they said.

As refugees unfamiliar with rights granted to people in this country, it would not have occurred to us to challenge something as powerful as a government - especially not the mighty United States of America. On our own, we would not have realized the government acted illegally, nor would we have known how to redress the wrong. Fortunately, our sponsors and hundred of others like them throughout the nation checked the laws and confronted their government. What a lesson we learned about American democracy and the privileges it guarantees.

Within weeks, refugees across America received letters, not quite apologizing, but at least partially rescinding the previous message. Enclosed with our letter was a check for the missing month's payment and a statement reminding us that the eighteen-month ruling was still in force. This letter was our thirty-day notice. Then, almost as an afterthought, the letter added that back payments would not be demanded. The letter did not solve the problem of how to finance our future, but at least we had time to find jobs or make other plans. It was a God-send.

However, before we learned about the government's altered decision, our sponsors met our immediate financial crunch so we could finish the current semester. Next, they helped us examine our financial obligations to see how much money we needed to complete our final year. When they learned how little we lived on, they explained how we could earn that much by working part-time and still be full-time students. They explained that we could provide an additional cushion against the lean winter earnings by working full-time that summer. We jumped at the opportunity. Vitou pumped gas, worked in an auto body shop, and started a yard maintenance business. I cleaned houses. Soon more customers wanted our services than we could accommodate.

Had we measured our lowly occupations and long hours against the lifestyle we'd known in prewar Cambodia, we would have felt the work was beneath us. Fortunately, well before our third summer in America, we'd learned a valuable lesson: any honest work is honorable work. By example, our sponsors showed us that manual labor need not be demeaning. The women did their own housework, and their children delivered newspapers or worked at fast-food outlets. Two of the men were dentists and three were professors, yet we saw them help in the kitchen, vacuum, wash windows, mow lawns, wax their cars, and put in gardens. In traditional Cambodia, no man of their stature would have considered such work.

During our final year of college, Vitou and I rented a postage-stamp-sized apartment in a rough neighborhood near campus and drove an old, donated Dodge Coronet, an ex-police car. We depended on that clunker to get us to and from our jobs. Vitou kept it running through sheer will power. I also worked in the school library where I earned $100 a week. With this patchwork of jobs we kept food on the table and the rent paid. Fortunately, financial aid from the school took care of tuition and book expenses.

Unlike his classmates who had lived and breathed mechanics since they were children and had extensive hands-on experience from tinkering with cars, motorcycles, and machines, Vitou didn't even know the English names for the tools. At first he spent hours at home memorizing and matching names with tool shapes and functions. Despite this handicap, one of Vitou's professors told a sponsor that Vitou would be an outstanding mechanic; he was one of the most dedicated and naturally gifted students the professor had ever seen. That encouraged Vitou, particularly since his first test scores had been so low he considered dropping out before the school kicked him out.

Initially we didn't understand much of what our teachers said in class. Tests never lasted long enough. By the time we digested the question and labored over the answer, other students were several questions ahead. Completing homework took us two or three times longer than it did most students. We used a dictionary to look up about half the words only to find the definition did not help; we had to look up those defining words too! Our lives consisted of little more than study, work, and sleep, with little of the latter. We worked longer and harder than we ever had under the Khmer Rouge, but despite setbacks, we knew we were mastering the material. That kept us going.

At long last the year ended; Vitou and I both graduated with honors! With associate degrees in hand, we wanted to put our hard-earned knowledge to work, if only someone would hire us. We wanted jobs in Silicon Valley where my sisters and brothers-in-law worked and where we could help care for my mother.

Some employers took one look at us, heard our accents, and said the job had been filled. It was discouraging. While awaiting replies to our many applications, we helped in the doughnut shop that Ken managed. Before long I found a job in my field, but Vitou could get only part-time work at a little airport, performing jobs far below his skill level.

Vitou, after training under Ken in his spare time, also became a Winchell's manager. He did quite well, but chafed under the disappointment of not being an airline mechanic. His grueling two-year effort seemed wasted. Even outstanding letters of recommendation from his former professors could not crack the system for him.

Vitou never quit applying but continued to bump against the same obstacle; he lacked work experience as a mechanic. Most of his fellow students had had some experience before they even enrolled in the aeronautical mechanics course. Some had been airplane mechanics in the military. Others had been employed in machine shops or auto repair garages. A few already worked at local airports and had taken the course just to advance their career potential.

His was the perennial dilemma many face: how to get a job in your field if you don't have experience and how to get experience if no one will hire you to work in your chosen career. The problem caused Vitou sleepless nights and left him demoralized, until he came up with a unique solution.

At first I thought he'd lost his senses. He joined the Navy Reserve! But Vitou had done his homework well. He learned that a person doesn't have to be an American citizen to enlist in its military, and that each branch needs airplane maintenance people. Recruiters said his college training assured him assignment in the reserves as an airplane mechanic. He also learned that major airlines apparently favor former military men; recruits know how to follow orders. Moffett Field, a navy installation, was near our home; that's why Vitou selected the Navy Reserve instead of another branch of the military.

After the drudgery and discipline of basic boot camp in southern California, Vitou moved to the reserve unit at Moffett Field where he worked on navy planes every duty weekend.

With ingenuity and persistence, Vitou finally landed a job with a major airline. He never lost sight of his long-term goal and had determined to do whatever was necessary to reach it, even if it meant temporarily taking jobs unrelated to his field and doing work he didn't like.

Vitou began his career as a mechanic on the night shift and has risen to Inspector on the day shift. Where did he find employment? At San Francisco International Airport, where he first saw the job he wanted in America and vowed, "That's what I want to be." And who is he working for? United Airlines, of course.

15   RELYING ON COUSINS

Chenda Poong:

Sampwa Moni and Tevi were more like sisters to me than cousins, so I had eagerly anticipated our reunion. Except for four years under the Khmer Rouge and our recent separation, our families had always lived together. I'd expected our friendship to resume where it left off eight months earlier, when their family left the refugee camp for America and ours did not. However, when I got to California, Tevi and Sampwa were strangers. It made me feel really bad inside that I no longer knew them. They weren't my Cambodian cousins; they seemed more like little Americans. It frightened me. I felt left out.

I both resented and envied their ability to talk and act like their new, American playmates. They moved with assurance in this foreign setting. Rota and I did not. It felt awkward to rely on our cousins; we weren't babies - I was eight and my brother ten. Not only must I look to Sampwa and Tevi for interpretation every time an American spoke, they had to show me how to live in a Western home.

Most embarrassing was the need to be shown how to use a Western-style toilet. I was only two and a half when we were forced from Phnom Penh, so I don't even remember the Asian style toilets we had in our home there. For the next five years we used holes dug behind our huts. When we got to California, everyone was preoccupied with settling in, and no one remembered that I would need instruction before using a toilet.

Alone in the bathroom, I puzzled over how to approach it - backside or face to the wall. I wondered why the toilet was shaped so strangely, why the hole was raised off the floor so high, and why it had such a large opening. The place where I thought my feet belonged was too narrow and rounded to be comfortable.

Cautiously I climbed up, toes curled over the edge of the seat and lowered myself toward the hole. I almost fell in. Trying again, I held onto the towel bar - conveniently placed for that purpose, I supposed. The bar certainly made it easier to remain suspended in a crouched position long enough to perform my duty. My aim was not too accurate, but I would, no doubt, get the hang of it before long, I told myself.

I don't know how many days went by before I mentioned the stupid design of American toilets to Sampwa. Since she was nearest my age, I felt most comfortable asking her for information. I asked, "How do you stand on these dumb toilets anyway?" "Very carefully," she chuckled, then kindly showed me how to sit on the toilet seat. My opinion of American bathrooms improved markedly after that lesson.

Later, Tevi told me that although she had soon adjusted to

Western-style toilets, she still felt reluctant to use the toilet paper. It was much too clean, soft, and pretty for such duty. What waste, extravagance even, to use those beautiful little white squares when, under the Khmer Rouge, all Cambodians had become accustomed to collecting leaves near the latrines for that function; it took only one or two painful mistakes before we had learned to avoid certain plants.

As much as I resented needing to consult Tevi and Sampwa about mundane aspects of living - which made me feel stupid - the change I minded most in our relationship was their attitude toward possessions. They had grown stingy. In eight months their family had acquired luxuries that Rota and I had never seen. We especially wanted to use their toys and bikes.

While we were growing up in Cambodia, where store-bought toys were almost non-existent, jealousy over other children's possessions was seldom a problem. Playthings were not something *owned*. If a child played with an object you liked, you could make one by using similar materials - bamboo, scraps of cloth, clay, or objects from around the house and garden. And our games of imagination did not require elaborate costumes or props. Old skirt lengths of material turned us into princesses, villains, witches, fashion designers, and much more. Slender bamboo became a magic wand, a stick horse, a king's scepter. Many activities centered on games of hide-and-seek, tug-o-war, tag, jump rope, hop-scotch, or tossing rocks at a line we drew in the dirt. We molded animals and made tea sets from mud, then baked them in the sun. We floated leaf boats down ditches, braided long grass blades, made baskets of bamboo and mats from reeds, and told stories.

In America, homemade toys no longer satisfied me or my brother because Sampwa and Tevi had *real* toys. We wanted to play with those wonderful things. They wouldn't share. "That's mine," they whined defensively each time we approached a toy. "It's rightfully mine. My sponsor gave it to me." Of course, our sponsors had given us toys too, and we didn't want to share them either.

Our cousins had more possessions than we because they'd been in America longer. But we had been given one thing better than their family had, a color television set. When Sampwa and Tevi got too bossy, we refused to let them come over to watch their favorite cartoons in color. At one point, we actually got into a fight over toys. We gave them the silent treatment, refused to go to their apartment, and kept them from ours.

Under the Khmer Rouge and later while escaping, the four of us had stuck together to protect each other and be lookouts for our extended family. We felt united. In the security of America, however, our solidarity began to crumble. Selfishness surfaced. I felt miserable.

Fortunately, our longing to be together soon outweighed our need to be possessive, and our friendship resumed. And it wasn't long before Rota's and my English improved enough that we no longer relied so heavily on Sam and Tev, as their American friends called them. Soon we, too, had shortened names that the American kids could more easily pronounce, Roth and Chenda.

A more equal friendship emerged as we adjusted to our surroundings and became less dependent. From this equality, a new closeness developed. Once more the four of us became best friends.

16 FANTASY VERSUS REALITY

Rasmei:

Several years before the Khmer Rouge enslaved us, I visited Paris with my husband. I'd also seen movies made in the West and observed many international tourists in Cambodia. Consequently, I thought I knew what to expect of Western countries and the people who lived there. In my mind these nations consisted almost entirely of big cities, tall buildings, great wealth, famous paintings, monumental statues and public buildings, beautiful homes in the suburbs, glamorous women, handsome men, easy living. I built a fantasy in my mind that America would have more of everything I'd seen in Europe's capital cities. After all, everyone knew America was rich, and California the richest of all. I almost expected to find streets paved with gold. Therefore, my first few months in the United States felt like a carnival ride of widely swinging emotions and sensations as I tried to sort out reality from fantasy.

My first reaction to America was disappointment. We, and a few dozen other refugees, landed at Hamilton Air Force Base north of San Francisco; there were no tall buildings in sight, no beautiful homes. The people looked ordinary.

As my young son stepped from the plane, it was evident to the social workers assigned to meet us, that something was wrong with his leg. They took us immediately to Letterman Hospital in San Francisco for X-rays to see if Rota's leg was broken; we already knew it was. My husband and the social worker accompanied Rota into the hospital while I remained in the car with our daughters, eight-year-old Chenda Poong and one-year-old Helena.

The first thing to impress me on our ride to the hospital was crossing the Golden Gate Bridge. It was spectacular! Just the sort of thing I expected of America. The San Francisco skyline was equally impressive. My hopes soared.

While waiting for the cast to be put on their brother's leg, the girls and I ducked whenever people walked past the car. I feared someone might talk to us, and I knew no English. But from our vantage point in the back seat, we admired the manicured lawns, carefully shaped shrubs, and beautifully tended flower gardens. These, too, matched my idea of what America should be. I was back in fantasy-land.

My high expectations for the good life in America had been

reinforced on our plane trip to California from Thailand. Flight attendants served fried chicken in cleverly constructed white, foam-plastic boxes. We ate the delicious contents of two boxes but saved the other three meals as gifts for my sisters and mother. Under the Khmer Rouge and while we were escaping from Cambodia, we seldom had enough to eat, so I wanted my relatives to share this wonderful food and have these beautiful, light-weight boxes. When we went through Customs, however, I felt frustrated that the officials took the food and self-hinging boxes from me and tossed them away! But at least this cavalier attitude toward food and the wonderful containers seemed yet another proof that America was the land of plenty.

The next day, one of our sponsors, Louise Kenner, came to Travis Air Force Base where we'd been taken after Rota's leg was set. Louise drove a large Chevrolet passenger van, verifying my opinion that in America everything is big. The trip to Davis, however, surprised me - no big cities. We traveled for an hour through farmland interspersed with communities on each side of the I-80 freeway. It hadn't occurred to me that America had farms. Cattle and sheep grazed on the hillsides as we drove through a small mountain range into the broad sweep of California's central valley. Orchards stretched for miles. Arrow-straight furrows ran across newly plowed soil. Huge tractors, not water buffalo or oxen, worked the fields. Still no big cities.

A reunion dinner awaited us and the rest of our relatives at a sponsor's home. Louise drove directly there rather than to our apartment. The Criddle home wasn't exactly the mansion I'd anticipated, but I could tell they were rich; they had wall-to-wall carpet. In Cambodia carpets were a sure sign of luxury.

It was great to be reunited with Teeda, Vitou, and my mother who had arrived a few days before we did. It felt even better to see Mearadey's family again. They had left for America eight months earlier. After greeting my relatives and shaking hands with all the Americans present, we sat down to eat something called taco salad - unusual flavors but quite good.

After the meal, our sponsors told Rota about the American custom of signing casts. Soon the cast on his leg sported names written in English and Cambodian. It seemed such a delightful, exotic custom.

A few sponsors spoke French, so we attempted three-way conversations in Cambodian, French, and English. Besides the thirteen members of our extended family, there must have been twenty or more Americans; too many for effective conversations, especially when everything had to pass through three languages.

Our sponsors' names were hard to pronounce and every American face looked so similar that I couldn't remember one from the other, but I could tell that our sponsors were friendly and wished us well. It took us several weeks to sort out their names and faces. Meanwhile, among ourselves we referred to them as, "the one with her hair in a chignon," "the woman who cries easily," "the man with glasses," "the woman with short curly hair," "the man who is balding," "the animal doctor," "the one whose son speaks French," and so on.

Following the meal and a short visit, Louise and her husband, Peter, took us to our new home. I was excited to learn that Mearadey's and Teeda's families lived near us, but disappointed we could not all live together as we had in prewar Cambodia.

After seeing the Criddles' large, five bedroom home and spacious garden, I could hardly wait to see the house the sponsors had prepared for us. I expected something similar, especially since Mearadey's letters to us in the refugee camp had described what a nice place had been provided for them. Instead of a beautiful home, we were taken to a small, second floor apartment. True, wall-to-wall carpet covered the floor, but the place was hardly grand. Used furniture filled the rooms adequately; pots, pans, and dishes lined the cupboards. The refrigerator was stocked with food. We had indoor plumbing, comfortable beds, closets filled with clothes, and even a television set. Compared to the bamboo huts we'd lived in for the previous five years this was a mansion. I knew I should be grateful, and I was, but what a let-down. Had Louise taken us directly to the apartment, I'd have been pleased, but unrealistic expectations surfaced when I saw our sponsor's home first. That and my many misconceptions about America and its wealth left me deflated.

A day or two later, Kathryn took me grocery shopping. Knowing better than I did that we must live frugally for years to come, she hoped to teach me how to shop economically. Our extended family had come from a middle-class lifestyle before the Khmer Rouge takeover, so it took some time to adjust my thinking to the reality that we could not immediately return to that status. I had no idea how much a dollar could buy or how we were to get the money we needed. The American movies I'd seen and novels I'd read never focused on employment or keeping to a schedule. I had yet to learn how hard successful Americans work and what long hours they put in. I had no concept of the lifestyle of the average American. I had not yet realized that scenes shown on the silver screen were about as similar to real life in America as a fairy tale, so I was ill prepared for that first shopping trip.

An American supermarket is something to behold. I wanted every food I'd not tasted in five years. I didn't know that mangos and papayas were expensive fruits and apples and bananas were not. Kathryn, not knowing how foreign canned fruits and vegetables would be to our taste, wanted me to stock up on these sale items. I could not believe rich Americans actually ate canned vegetables and fruits when the stores overflowed with fresh produce.

Language and cultural differences proved major barriers on that shopping trip. As I eyed expensive products, I finally noticed that Kathryn quietly tried to steer me to less expensive choices. She attempted to point out the difference between "five

USA Spring 1980 - Chenda Peach, baby Helena, Roth, Chenda, Sam, Tevi

Christmas 1990 - Chenda, Sam, Tevi, Chenda Peach, Seri, Helena

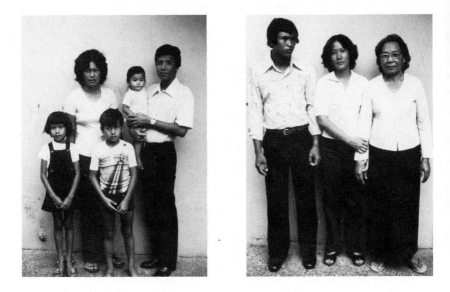

USA Spring 1980 - Back: Rasmei, Helena, Leng
                        Front: Chenda and Roth (whose cast was recently removed)

USA Spring 1980 - Vitou, Teeda and Ean Bun

USA Spring 1980 - Tevi, Ken, Mearadey, Sam, and Chenda Peach in front

Prewar Cambodia - Back: Ean Bun's 3 brothers (2 killed by Khmer Rouge) youngest lives
    in France   Front: Rasmei, Samol's mother (still in Cambodia), Ean Bun, Mearadey,

Fall 1980 - Back: Mearadey, Ean Bun, Kathryn
Front: Roth, Sam, Helena, Chenda
Courtesy photo by Cindy O'Dell, *The Davis Enterprise*

July 24, 1986 - Following Vitou and Teeda's citizenship ceremony:
Ean Bun, Teeda, Vitou, Joan

Prewar Cambodia - Vitou (back row center wearing hat) with friends; his only photo from Cambodia.

USA Spring 1980 - Vitou

1984 - Anne and Vitou at doughnut shop

Prewar Cambodia - Back: Ken, Mearadey, Rasmei and relatives (2 killed by Khmer Rouge)
Front: Sam, Tevi and other relatives with Roth front center.

Christmas 1990 - Back: Leng, Samol, Ken, Tevi, Mearadey, Rasmei, Soorsdey, Teeda,
Chenda, Sam, Vitou, Roth
Middle: Chenda Peach, Little Grandma Houy
Yek Ngak, Big Grandma Ean Bun, Seri
Front: Helena, Laura, Andrew

USA Spring 1980 - Teeda, Ean Bun, Mearadey, Rasmei

Christmas 1990 - Soorsdey, Teeda, Mearadey, Rasmei, Ean Bun seated

Christmas 1990 - Ean Bun's Daughters: Teeda, Mearadey, Soorsdey, Rasmei

Christmas 1990 - Ean Bun's Son's-in-law: Vitou, Leng, Ken, Samol

December 1990 - Ken's mother arrives from Cambodia: Houy Yek Ngak with Ean Bun

Summer 1990 - Andrew and Laura

1990 - Chenda's high school portrait   1990 - The Boy Cousins: Roth holding Andrew

for one dollar" and "one for five dollars."

Before leaving the apartment to go shopping, Kathryn had helped me prepare a list of basic foods we would need. She tried to keep me to that list. I wanted to ignore it and buy whatever caught my fancy. I'm sure she thought I'd never learn, but she didn't act annoyed. Understanding my curiosity about all the exotic items on the shelves such as peanut butter, racks of prewrapped bread, pet food, strange looking kitchen gadgets, and dozens of soap brands, Kathryn patiently pushed our cart along and let me browse.

As we entered the cosmetics aisle, I recognized Max Factor products, a brand well known in Cambodia. That aisle drew me like a magnet. My eyes settled on a compact. Suddenly it seemed vitally important to own it. I don't know why, but I felt I needed it. I couldn't explain the urge to Kathryn. It wasn't even the make-up, I realized, I'd just fallen in love with that cute little pink plastic box with a mirror inside. Looking back now, this need seems irrational, but five years of Spartan living under the Khmer Rouge was reason enough for such desires, I guess. Kathryn waited patiently while I admired the lovely box. Gently she explained that perhaps with the little money we had to spend, we should concentrate on basic foods before we bought other things. Fortunately, before I made a complete fool of myself, it occurred to me that we couldn't afford cosmetics. The realization that we were poor was finally sinking in. Kathryn and I turned to more practical selections, but my thoughts lingered in the cosmetic aisle.

Movies and magazines had pictured California as a pleasantly warm place, but when we arrived in mid-March I could not warm up. When our sponsors learned of my problem, they loaned me an electric blanket. I suspect my reaction was the shock of cultural adjustment as much as the actual cold, but after getting that wonderful electric blanket I hated to climb out of my warm, cozy bed each morning. I felt safe there. In contrast, the world beyond my bedroom door left me insecure and confused. Fortunately, Mearadey and Ken had already confronted most situations we had yet to face. They and our sponsors helped us over the rough spots of adjustment.

Shortly after our arrival, Ken and Mearadey, Vitou and Teeda, Leng and I met with our sponsors to discuss long-range goals and how to make them a reality. I'm sure our sponsors will never know how difficult it was for us to agree to start a housecleaning service as a way to augment our welfare income while we mastered English and established ourselves in America. As they suggested options that paid well for hours expended, we saw the reasonableness of the housecleaning suggestion. It offered flexible hours so most of us could go to school. Unlike traditional jobs, we could fill in for each other when needed. It paid well for unskilled labor, and the work required little English. Best of all, we could launch our own business with only a few dollars in start-up costs.

The sponsors had a friend, David Smith, who was willing to teach us how to clean windows professionally and another friend, Janet Morris, willing to show us which products to use and how to clean to American standards. What our sponsors couldn't know was how demeaning that work seemed to people from our culture and former social standing. We'd once had servants to do this kind of work. But we reasoned among ourselves that this was America, not Cambodia; the norms were different here. We would have to adapt or give up our dreams of a better future.

While still in the Thai refugee camp, Teeda and I had been shocked when Mearadey first told us that sponsors had scrubbed our two apartments, washed the windows, and cleaned the toilets in anticipation of our arrival. These women were wives of professional men. We found it hard to believe they actually did such work, until we saw them cleaning their own homes. Our sponsors' ways often puzzled us. Obviously they didn't consider manual labor beneath them. Nor were their husbands above window washing, or dish washing for that matter. Vitou told me how surprised he'd been to see Professor Criddle in grubby clothes, working on a boat motor in his carport. He said, "He must be a rich man. Why doesn't he just buy a new motor or hire someone to fix it?"

At first, all of us participated in the housecleaning business, but as our husbands became more involved in career training courses and Teeda and Vitou became full-time students, the rapidly expanding cleaning service fell to Mearadey and me. Although it was not our favorite thing to do, we took pride in doing it well. The women we worked for became our friends. It surprised us to find some of them chose to clean alongside us. No one treated us as though we were servants or demeaned us for the work we did. On the contrary, they expressed gratitude for our help and paid us well. Many of these women lived in elegant homes like those I'd seen in movies, yet they seemed to consider us equals. With her earnings, Mearadey bought the family's first new car. Our clients seemed almost as proud of her accomplishment as we were.

That cleaning business proved to be a valuable experience. It taught me that in America your worth is measured by the person you are, not the work you do. I saw first-hand that when these rich women weren't helping us clean, they had other work to do, often volunteer work. They were not idle and indulgent as I thought rich Americans would be. Some women said that when they were young they, too, had cleaned for other people. They'd worked as secretaries or clerks in stores. Several had put themselves through college or helped put their husbands through. Even their children worked at fast food restaurants, delivered newspapers, or took babysitting jobs. We'd never met people so obsessed with being productive. Their pride in self-reliance rather than in what we called "maintaining face" was an alien, but refreshing concept to us.

Just when I'd adjusted to the reality of life in America and not the fairy-tale, movie version I'd imagined, an unexpected turn of events made it possible for us to move into the Criddle home a mere five months after we arrived in the country. Since Joan and Dick would be working out of the country for eighteen months, they asked if our extended family wanted to rent their big house. They knew of our dream to live under the same roof again. They had even helped us look for such housing but with no success. Either we couldn't afford the rent, or people were unwilling to lease to a group of thirteen, or they took one look at our Cambodian faces and found excuses why the property was no longer available. Criddles let us live in their home for less than we paid for our three separate apartments - so, I got to live in a dream house after all.

As it had been in prewar Cambodia, watching TV movies together in Dick and Joan's house provided our favorite evening entertainment. We each had our spot in the family room where we always sat. Mearadey claimed the right-hand corner of the couch; I sat next to her, and Teeda next to me; we three sisters frequently needed to share a box of tissues during sad parts of the movies. Vitou sat next to Teeda. The others squeezed onto the couch, lounged on the floor, or claimed chairs. We loved the mini-series *Shogun*; each evening we rushed through dinner in order to finish before the movie started. As usual, Ken sat on a straight-backed chair at Mearadey's side and gave us a running commentary of the dialogue; his English was the best.

I still love TV movies; but like many other immigrants I had to learn to separate movie fantasy from American reality before I could fully appreciate or adjust to life in this new homeland.

17 A SAN FRANCISCO OUTING

Teeda:

San Francisco. The mere sound of the words filled me with anticipation. Watching out the apartment window, I saw the car drive up and its keys handed to my brother-in-law. In the flurry of preparation that followed, we never paused to consider how seven of us were going to fit in that little car for our first trip to San Francisco.

Only weeks before, I'd stepped hesitatingly from the plane onto American soil, a refugee in an alien land. Being reunited with a sister and her family whom I thought I'd never see again was cause for happy tears - a time to rejoice. Even more amazing, thirteen members of our extended family were now safe and together again, a miracle demanding celebration. But how to celebrate when we were stripped of worldly possessions?

Then a thoughtful sponsor, Kathryn Gardner, offered the use of her car for the day. "Wouldn't the family like to go some place just for fun and relaxation?"

Would we! Fun had been almost non-existent in our lives for five years, and relaxation would be rare for years to come as we struggled to establish ourselves in this new land.

For nearly four years we'd survived as slaves of the Khmer Rouge, then struggled another year to escape and reach the safety of America. How we hungered for fun and a change of pace, if only for a day. My mother stayed home with five grandchildren. We other adults took ten-year-old Sampwa Moni with us. I don't remember how she earned that privilege.

Hoping for light traffic, the seven of us began our adventure near dawn on a beautiful spring Sunday. In Cambodia before the Khmer Rouge takeover, my oldest sister and her husband had been accomplished drivers, but in America, Mearadey had passed her driving test just days before our trip. Her husband, Ken, had only a learner's permit. Excitedly we piled in the car and were on our way, only vaguely aware of the many traffic laws we were breaking.

Ken drove. It is almost a straight shot down I-80 from Davis to San Francisco. That was good, because our map-reading ability was almost as limited as our English. One and a half hours later, Ken pulled to a stop on a nearly deserted street in San Francisco's Chinatown. Sleepy-eyed shopkeepers were unlocking doors and positioning awnings as we left the car.

Laughing and gawking, we roamed for hours, enjoying everything. Eager tourists buying baubles rubbed shoulders with neighborhood housewives squeezing produce. Butchers shooed rambunctious children and pesky flies. The sights, smells, sounds, and jostling crowds brought fond memories of Cambodia in its prewar days.

This glorious day flew by too quickly. Shadows crept high up building fronts on the east side of streets, leaving the shops below in deep shade. Time to start home. To our dismay, we saw that cars now filled every available parking space. We had no idea where we'd parked all those hours ago. We weren't sure of the car's make, license plate number, or even its color. Laughing at our carelessness, we concluded that we might have to wait until the streets emptied. By default, the car remaining should be Kathryn's.

My niece spared us the embarrassment of having to wait. She saw a sweater that looked familiar in the back window of a parked car. However, we all wore newly donated clothes, so we weren't sure if the sweater really belonged to her. After consultation, we decided that this was the right car, especially since the key fit.

Happy but tired from the day's excitement, we started home. With six back seat drivers, it's surprising that Ken eventually found the freeway entrance - a task made even more difficult by heavy traffic.

One thing people have always admired about our family is our enjoyment in being together. Given half a chance, we know how to have fun. This day was no exception. We spent most of the drive home laughing at what country bumpkins we had been. We were having such a good time that Ken failed to note that he was going seventy-five miles per hour in a fifty-five mph zone.

Oh, we'd all noticed for some time that a car behind us flashed a red light. Not knowing any better, Ken ignored it until the car pulled alongside, and with a bull horn aimed our direction, a patrolman bellowed for Ken to pull over.

We were panic stricken. Previous experience with the Khmer Rouge, who killed people on almost any pretext, left us deathly afraid of officials. Would we be jailed? Would they kick us out of America? What would happen to Kathryn's car? Like irresponsible children we'd betrayed a trust. How could we ever face her?

Then an added realization struck home, Ken was driving with six passengers on just a learner's permit. Oh, the laws we'd broken. The shame we felt.

Standing behind our vehicle, the officer wrote down the car's license number. I couldn't decide which looked more menacing, his huge holstered gun or the grim look on his face.

The sun seemed to leave the sky; our future looked black. America had given us a chance at a new life and we'd failed. The effervescence of the day evaporated in the brief moments it took the officer to reach the driver's side of the car.

As Ken rolled down the window, Mearadey, ever the quick thinking one in a crisis, handed him her driver's license to give to the officer. The stern-faced patrolman scrutinized the pictureless, temporary license and asked a few questions. It took him only a minute to realize that we were scared silly, were new to America, had almost no command of the language, and were contrite to the core.

Kindly, slowly, he explained that we had been going too fast, there were seven people in the car and only four seat belts. . . . Then he handed Ken a traffic ticket and explained that we must pay a fine for speeding.

We couldn't believe our good luck! We were free to go; the

officer trusted us to pay the money later. Suddenly the day
seemed sunny once more. The guillotine no longer hung over
our heads. Now Kathryn need never know how irresponsible
we'd been. Our secret was safe.

Admonishing Ken to watch his speed, the officer waved us on,
never guessing that *Mearadey* is not a man's name.

18 MY FIRST EASTER

Roth:

Fortunately, by Easter I'd overcome my reluctance to step on
lawns. When I arrived in America with my family a few weeks
earlier, I'd been astonished that every yard, park, and even
school grounds had neatly edged, carefully cut grass. Another
surprise came when I saw these manicured lawns routinely
watered, something unnecessary in tropical Cambodia. Every
lawn seemed beautifully kept, so I decided they must be just to
look at, not step on. Not knowing American customs, and not
wanting to offend, I made it a rule to keep off all grass - until I
saw Americans regularly walking, playing, and even picnicking on
it.

My leg still sported its new cast that first Easter. I had
broken it in the Thai refugee camp playing soccer with friends
shortly before we left for America. If our playing field had been
smooth, like the lawns we saw in the parks in Davis, there would
have been no rock for me to trip over. But there was, and I fell,
and my leg had hurt terribly. Friends helped me hobble back to
my parents in the refugee barracks.

My father had been quite sure I'd broken my leg, but he
asked me not to let anyone know. Quietly he explained why he
didn't dare report my accident to the camp authorities; we could
not afford to miss our best chance of being accepted for

immigration to America. We'd already survived two dangerous escapes from Cambodia. After our first escape, soldiers forced us back from Thailand, along with thousands of others classed as *illegal aliens*. After the second escape, Thai soldiers sent us to the Buriram refugee camp where we lived for five long, monotonous months while awaiting sponsorship to a third country.

At last, American sponsors had been arranged and our papers processed. We were scheduled to be in America within days, but not if we had medical problems. If my broken leg kept us from our scheduled flight, who knew if or when we'd get another chance. I was only ten, but agreed to maintain silence about the break despite the pain. My father could count on me to not even limp when we boarded the bus for Bangkok. However, when we arrived at Hamilton Air Force Base north of San Francisco a few days later, a social worker spotted a limp I could no longer hide. At Letterman General Hospital near Golden Gate Bridge, X-rays were taken and my leg put in a bright white cast.

I was just learning to get around well with crutches when our sponsors told us about the upcoming Easter Egg Hunt in the city park. My cousins Tev and Sam had been in America for most of a year, yet even their English was not good enough for them to understand why anyone would want to hide hundreds of candy eggs in a park just so a bunch of kids could find them. But it sounded great to us.

Saturday morning we arrived at Central Park early. To our disappointment, early arrival was not an advantage. A flimsy yellow ribbon around the edge of the park was as near the grass as we were allowed. The adults said that everyone had to stay behind the ribbon and wait for some signal. Since we couldn't get a head start by arriving early, we did the next best thing. My sister and I and our cousins used the time to scan the area.

From behind the ribbon, we began spotting the candy eggs.

Other kids foolishly pointed at the eggs they saw, letting everyone know where to look. Not us. We kept our hands in our pockets, but since we spoke in Cambodian, we didn't have to keep our voices lowered. Soon the four of us had agreed on who would go where. This was not the first or the last time we enjoyed the benefit of using a *secret* language; it almost made up for the disadvantage of our limited ability to speak or understand English. The egg hunt was serious business as far as we were concerned. We had survived the Khmer Rouge years by scrounging and competing for any extra food; our lives had depended on it.

When the organizers signalled the start of the hunt, I was glad that well-mown grass no longer acted as a deterrent to me. Nor did my broken leg slow me down much. One little kid bent toward an egg I'd spotted earlier. I felt it was rightfully mine; I'd targeted it from the sidelines. No scruples kept me from snatching it before he could. He looked startled but didn't complain; that reinforced my opinion that he knew it was really mine.

We were so greedy and aggressive. It is amazing the organizers didn't kick the four of us out. Years later, a sponsor told us that when she was growing up in northern Utah, merchants put their store's name on some eggs. Those eggs could be redeemed for cash. It's a good thing that that wasn't the practice in Davis in 1980 or the other kids would really have gone eggless!

It was years before we learned that Easter was the celebration of a religious event, that Christians did not see the egg hunt as the holiday's focus. It certainly was for us. All we knew was that Americans had this great holiday and we were all for it. We never questioned why they hid eggs, why the celebration took place, or why it was repeated annually. The holiday's point escaped us, but not its candy.

19 PERFORMING

Rasmei:

One of our funniest, most embarrassing experiences happened shortly after we came to America. Kathryn invited Mearadey, Teeda, and me to attend a women's meeting at her church. She was making a presentation about sponsoring refugees and telling our family's story.

Apparently she told Mearadey about the program the week before and asked if the three of us would help her by doing "something Cambodian" for the group. Although Mearadey's English was better than ours, she couldn't be sure she had understood Kathryn, but she agreed.

Mearadey is such a tease that when she told us about performing she laughed so much we felt sure she was joking. She kept insisting she wasn't, but her face told us otherwise. We refused to take her seriously because it seemed such an unlikely thing to be asked to do.

Seldom would Cambodians perform in public unless they were professional entertainers. It is foreign to our culture. We try not to focus attention on ourselves; we try to blend in, be part of the group. Females, especially, are taught to be demure and remain in the background when in public.

Mearadey said Kathryn suggested we sing. That really made us laugh. Well, we didn't believe her, so we didn't prepare anything. Even if we had believed her, we would have had no idea what to prepare. Occasionally during the week Mearadey badgered us about it, but we just kidded back with her. Kathryn picked us up in time for the meeting and said our part would be right after she finished. That's when Teeda and I finally believed Mearadey. I think that is when Mearadey first believed it herself. Still we didn't prepare.

To the thirty or so women at the meeting, Kathryn told our story, wiping away tears as she did so. Soon the entire audience was crying. Everyone responded emotionally except the three of us. This was the first time we'd heard someone tell about our experience as though it were a story. It struck us as funny. Perhaps because we were nervous, we began to giggle. We kept poking each other in the ribs trying to make the others stop. It didn't work.

We could not understand why these women, who didn't even know us, thought our story so sad. We felt just the opposite. We'd lived that terrible experience, which at the time was awful, but we'd survived. We were lucky! We'd made it.

By the time we went to the meeting in our nice, donated, western-style clothes, we felt great. Life seemed good. We had been treated really well in America and were pleased with ourselves and our fortunate situation. Just a few months before, Mearadey had thought we were dead; we thought we'd never see her again. Miraculously, we were safe and reunited. We felt excited and happy to be in America, a land we'd only dreamed about. We didn't dwell on the horrors of the past. Yet here, a roomful of strangers were sad enough to be in tears. It was awkward; we weren't accustomed to seeing such open displays of emotion.

As children, Cambodians are taught to suppress feelings. We learned that by making our face a mask of neutrality, we could maintain privacy in our pain. But even more important, in our culture it is considered rude to burden others with our sadness and childish to publish our gladness. Also, superstition plays a part; if bad spirits learn about the happiness they might do something to destroy it. Being open about good things that happen just invited trouble. Bad things or sad things openly displayed only delighted the demons and tempted them to make things worse. In addition, most Cambodians believe in reincarnation and Karma - believing that the way we lived in a former life determines what happens to us in this life. Those who were good before enjoy an even better life this time. The wicked or lazy will get what they deserve the next time.

So although Cambodians didn't know what we had done to deserve to be treated worse than slaves by our own countrymen, most Cambodians who survived the Khmer Rouge regime felt a sense of collective guilt for some unknown despicable deed in a past life. Many still carry that sense of shame. Others feel guilty for having survived when loved ones did not. We were raised with a fatalistic philosophy of life; perhaps we had tempted fate and others suffered the consequences. Or perhaps those who died were the lucky ones. "Why," some asked, "wasn't I lucky too? Then I would be free of this suffering." We had been trained so well in being stoic that many Cambodians never once cried during the years of servitude, not even when they witnessed the murder of loved ones.

Under the Khmer Rouge, inappropriate giggling became a telling sign that a person was under stress. Perhaps that's what happened to us at the women's meeting, but I don't think so. My sisters and I genuinely thought it was funny that strangers cried for us at a time we felt so lucky.

When Kathryn finished, she turned to us. Dutifully, we went to the front but could think of nothing to do. She suggested we sing a typical Cambodian song, but none came to mind.

Cambodian girls often hold hands as they walk along singing a little ditty. Whispering to each other, we finally decided to try one of those from our childhood. We told Teeda to start. She did fine until our giggles began again. We could hardly control them enough to join her. We finished somehow but it was really awkward.

We are more westernized now and realize our experience that night was the result of different cultural expectations. Unlike Cambodians, many Americans seem to enjoy standing out in a crowd; they are accustomed to seeing members of the group perform for each other. They even take lessons to develop performing talents. Western kids get lots of encouragement and practice. In contrast, Asian children would likely be punished for inappropriate behavior - for trying to show off - if they did the same things. Americans have pranced around in front of admiring relatives since they could walk. Parents applaud their baby's first efforts to move up and down with the rhythm. Kindergarten kids have Show and Tell time. American children are in dramatic productions, give reports at school, and perform at music recitals. Apparently it is no big deal for them.

With effort, we've even learned some of that openness ourselves since coming to America. Teeda, especially, and my own children and my nieces give speeches, conduct meetings, and otherwise perform for an audience. Helena was student-body president of her elementary school. At work, we adults have learned management and leadership skills, but we still feel a little uncomfortable exercising them.

Even at the time of the women's meeting, my sisters and I realized that Kathryn would never have asked us to perform had she understood how impossible it would be for us. To get up and sing or dance for strangers seemed shameful behavior, especially for married women, perhaps like asking a conservative American woman to do a striptease for a crowd. We could have said no, and we should have. Mearadey should have explained to Kathryn that Cambodian women would not be comfortable performing; we would feel brazen. That option never occurred to Mearadey, nor would it to any of us. To deny Kathryn's request would have seemed equally brazen.

When a sponsor asked us to do something, we just did it. Or at least we tried. To decline was unthinkable. We could not refuse them anything, even if we didn't know exactly what they asked or why. They had given us new life; we could never repay the debt of gratitude we felt. By then we trusted they'd not withdraw support or love if we didn't comply, so it is hard to explain our feelings; it was just something we had to do. But, of course, when the time actually came, we weren't able; our embarrassment was too keen.

When we got home that night, we were still laughing, each blaming the others for not doing their part, and for keeping us from doing ours. Even now, when we think of that incident, we start laughing all over again. It reminds us how far we've come, in twelve years, in adapting to American ways.

No one who saw us last Christmas (1990) would ever believe we had once been so shy. Soorsdey, Samol, and their daughter, Seri, came from Canada. It was the first Christmas our entire family had been together, our eleventh Christmas in America. On that cherished occasion we especially enjoyed this great Western holiday, one of our favorites. We four sisters and our teenaged daughters bought party dresses for the celebration. One night, in an especially silly mood, we all dressed up in our finery and danced around the room to taped music. Even the men joined us for awhile. We sang, danced, and clowned while Teeda's husband got it all on video.

We were even brash enough to send a copy of the tape to our relatives still in Cambodia. We feared they might disown us; instead, they loved it. They've written back asking for more of the same. Obviously things are changing even in that tradition-bound land.

20 VITOU
By Anne House

The first thing I noticed about my skinny new student was his teeth. They were beautiful.

I taught adult education courses that summer of 1980. Most students didn't know English well but struggled diligently to pass the high school equivalency exams to get a GED (General Education Diploma). Other students studied for the history and

government test which was required before they could become
American citizens. Members of this heterogeneous group
included Pakistanis, East Indians, and Mexicans, but many of my
newest students had fled the current troubled spot on the globe,
Southeast Asia. All my foreign students seemed grateful and
happy to be in America. They were adjusting well and appeared
healthy, but years of poverty and lack of medical attention had
taken a toll. Most were thin. All had bad teeth; the exception
was Vitou.

Vitou Mam was almost twenty-two years old. He had been in
America only three months but had already taken English
immersion courses. He must have studied well, because his
English was fairly good. I soon learned he had recently
experienced the horrors of war and slavery in Cambodia and the
squalor and frustration of life in a refugee camp in Thailand.
After years of laboring for the Khmer Rouge, he thrilled at the
prospect of controlling his own life, of making his own decisions.
For Vitou, being successful was a top priority.

Weeks passed before I realized that he rode his bike every
day from Davis, at least a twenty-mile round trip. He rose early,
peddled north along the shoulder of busy Highway 113, then
each afternoon retraced his dangerous route in the wilting
summer heat of California's central valley. When I learned
about his bike rides, I knew it wasn't just those pretty teeth, but
his punishing inner drive that made this student different.

Vitou was in my second period, a class for those interested in
gaining a high school diploma. However, it could be considered
an English-as-a-Second-Language class since most of the students
were from foreign countries. These classes, under the direction
of the Woodland Unified School District, met upstairs in a very
old but graceful brick building. Each day I watched as Vitou,
always on time, locked his bike and bounded up the grand
marble stairs with his load of books. In class, he soon acquired
the nickname R2-V2, a variation of the name of the robot R2-

D2 in the popular *Star Wars* movie. Ironically, Vitou spoke better English than most of my students, although he had been in America the shortest time.

On his first day in class, I offered him a doughnut, and we discussed his future goals. The doughnuts marked a classroom celebration for a couple from Pakistan who had become American citizens the previous day. With the privilege of citizenship came a time-honored tradition in our class - buying doughnuts for everyone. Vitou ate the doughnut while I explained to him the requirements to be met for American citizenship.

His much desired, long term goal was citizenship, he said, but his immediate goal was passing the high school proficiency exam and improving his English. He did not want these things casually or when they became convenient. He wanted them *now*. Whatever hardship it took, he would bear it. I set him up with appropriate courses and gave him his books. What drive he had, this new student of mine! He had no money or connections - just drive.

During one of our early discussions, he confided, almost sheepishly, that he wanted to be a mechanic, an airplane mechanic if possible. A long road stretched ahead of him before he could hope to reach that goal; there were many classes to attend and lessons to memorize.

Vitou soon felt at home with our classroom family and became a valued member. The students readily accepted each other, not only because they enjoyed new friendships, but because they learned so much from one another. Often we had round-table discussions to encourage their emerging English skills. From those group conversations we learned many startling things about Vitou.

First, we learned that his family and friends had nicknamed him The Smuggler. His previous experiences as a teenaged soldier and hunter taught him to travel undetected in the jungle. Before escaping from Cambodia, he made several secret crossings into Thailand. He carried valuables for sale or barter and returned to his family with life-saving food, medicines, other supplies, and vital information about safe escape routes. Although he spoke modestly in class about his exploits, these dangerous crossings sounded like a script out of a secret-agent movie. Although many students had come from impoverished countries, none had experienced such dangers of daily living as this student described.

Vitou explained to the group how best to hide jewels, silver, gold, and other small valuables when traveling to and from the border so that thieves, greedy border guards, or pocket-lining soldiers would not detect them. Once he'd hidden a beeswax-wrapped diamond in his ear; it looked like dirty earwax to the thieves. Jewels coated with pine pitch and knotted in unkempt hair had passed for snarls. During his escape from Cambodia, he swallowed his mother-in-law's large diamond ring when gun-toting soldiers surprised the group in the mountain pass. He told the wide-eyed students - who hadn't dared to ask - simply, "I retrieved the ring a few days later."

Of all the colorful and exciting stories Vitou told the group that summer, one has been my favorite. One day he revealed that he knew how to make poisoned darts and spear points to hunt wild game in the jungle. He described the procedure for making the poison for the tips from the venomous head of a cobra - first you had to catch a cobra. In his increasingly good English Vitou kept the group enthralled with his description of striking the cobra very fast with a short, flexible stick.

This one confession - that he could make poison for darts - always struck me as funny. I have taught fourth graders for many years, and each year, tongue-in-cheek, I tell them, "You can't frighten me! After all, *I* once had a student who could make poisoned darts from cobras' heads and even *he* didn't dare shoot me."

One day in class I knew that even this brave young man must have received a fright by the events that transpired. I was instructing the students, facing the grand expanse of wall-to-wall windows, when suddenly - *boom! crash!* Glass from the shattered windows showered the room; students screamed, and I dove under the table with the rest of them. Our school had been the target of a drive-by shooting. The glass-littered floor altered my students' idea of America's supposed safety.

Throughout that hot summer, day in and day out, Vitou came faithfully and studied diligently. When he felt ready to take one of the five tests - math, writing, reading, science, social studies - we reviewed it together; then I gave him a practice test and wished him luck as he headed for Woodland Senior High School for the official exam. He seldom passed the exam on the first try and took some tests many times. Occasionally, he returned to class so discouraged that my heart ached for him.

I knew it was only his English that held him back. He was smart - very smart. He was dedicated, the most dedicated student I'd ever known. Unfortunately, the English language has many subtleties and idioms that can trip even the best book-learned student. Vitou merely redoubled his efforts and studied harder. I remember his beautiful, neat handwriting. His notebooks soon filled with new vocabulary, phrases, and math problems. His English dictionary showed heavy use.

In September he left the Woodland school for work and night school courses. Within a year he'd passed all the high school equivalency tests and enrolled in a community college.

After he left my class, I missed him but knew he would be successful. Vitou was an outstanding human being - kind, quiet, humble, smart, and goal oriented. Occasionally, I learned of his progress through one of his sponsors, my dentist. Apparently, he and Teeda were on the high road to the American Dream and driving fast. Eighteen months before, they had eked out a miserable existence in a country torn by war and fear. Now they

were college students living in a rented home and driving an old
battered car, like so many other students their age.

I next saw Vitou at a New Year's Eve dance. There I finally
met his wife. Teeda was stylish, pretty, and spoke remarkably
good English. I couldn't help thinking to myself, what a
handsome couple! No one would guess from looking at them
the horrors they've seen.

When they moved from the area, I lost all contact with Vitou
and Teeda. But every year, when I have a new set of fourth
grade students, I tell them Vitou's story. They laugh about the
poisoned darts. They gasp at the swallowed ring. And they
invariably yell, "Oh, gross!" when I tell how he retrieved it.
However, they always understand how passionate I am about this
young Cambodian refugee who valued education so much that
he rode his bike each day in the sweltering heat *just to be in
school* - just to have the privilege of learning. They know I
expect no less from them.

This story could end here, but it doesn't. Four years after
Vitou left, I attended a training seminar in a small town south of
San Francisco with three colleagues. Fearing we'd missed our
turn-off, we finally decided to leave the freeway and ask
directions or consult our map more carefully.

We headed for a nearby gas station, but I said, "No, let's go to
that doughnut shop where we can sit and relax while we find out
where we are." We entered Winchell's (somewhere in the Bay
Area, three hours from home, feeling surrounded by four million
strangers) and selected a table near the window. My friends
settled in while I approached the counter to order four
doughnuts, four milks, and good directions. A man in a white
apron emerged from the back and stopped in his tracks. The
way he stared made me feel uncomfortable.

"Mrs. House?" he asked timidly. Startled, I looked around to
see if he was addressing someone else. I didn't know this heavy

set, Asian man.   Then he smiled, . . . those teeth.   Those beautiful teeth!

"Vitou!" I shouted, finally recognizing him.   "Vitou! R2-V2!" He bolted around the counter and grabbed me in a bear hug. What a coincidence; we could hardly believe it.

Vitou brought out the best doughnuts in the shop and sat with us.   Catching up on events since we'd last met, I soon learned that after much schooling and menial night jobs, he was well on his way to fulfilling his dream of becoming an aeronautical mechanic.   (Not long after that meeting he began working for United Airlines.)

That's the last time I saw Vitou and, just as it had been at our first meeting, we munched doughnuts and discussed his plans. We exchanged addresses, I snapped photos, he gave us directions to our conference, and we said our warm goodbyes. I still remember him standing in the Winchell's parking lot clad in a baker's apron, waving and smiling that wonderful smile, with all those beautiful, straight, white teeth.

21 SAMPLING HIGH SCHOOL

Teeda:

When the adult school I'd been attending for two months closed for the summer, I told my sponsors that, until Fremont opened again in September, I wanted to learn about the history and customs of this country I now called home.

Although I was a few years older than the high school kids, I looked young, so the sponsors got permission for me to audit summer courses in American history and social studies at Davis Senior High School.   They explained to the teachers that I probably couldn't participate fully, but I would learn something about history and social issues and have valuable exposure to hearing and speaking English.

I did learn quite a bit about the subject matter, and my English comprehension improved, but the real education came from observing American teenagers and seeing how the education system worked in this country.   The classroom casualness took some getting used to - in fact, it shocked me.

With time, however, I learned to appreciate the genuine exchange of ideas and the ability students had to ask questions and receive thoughtful answers.   What a contrast to Cambodia, where teachers dispensed information and students absorbed it. To ask questions was considered rude.   Teachers there demanded and received the highest respect and deference. Original answers weren't wanted; *good* students were those who parroted back accurately what the teacher told them.

Eager to learn, I walked into the bookcase-lined classroom the first day.   I almost walked out again.   I thought I'd come to the wrong place.   Chairs seemed haphazardly placed around the room, and students lounged on the sofa and chairs.   The kids acted friendly but generally ignored me, which was fine with me. I didn't want to try speaking English more than necessary. Apparently, students could sit where they wanted, so I took a seat in an out-of-the-way corner to take in the amazing scene.

A boy, wearing no shoes - but obviously not poor - walked in. He took a handful of books off the shelf, plopped them on the floor, and sat on them!   From across the room, another boy tossed him a football right over my head.   As they joked and threw the ball back and forth, I felt sure I was in the wrong room.   Could this really be a classroom in the United States?   It seemed weird.   Could learning possibly take place here?

I felt particularly outraged by the disregard of books.   In my country books were very expensive and, therefore, precious and treated with respect.   No classroom I had known contained so many beautiful books.   I took one from the shelf while I waited for the teacher to arrive.   The quality was remarkable, just like those in the pile the boy still sat on. It had a sturdy binding and a full color photograph on the cover. The slick inside pages had colored photos, diagrams, and graphs. The printing was of the highest quality. Incredible.

I had owned one book in Cambodia, a dictionary, a child's dictionary that my brother-in-law Leng brought as a gift for me from his trip to England. One book. I treasured it. I kept it in my room and allowed no one to touch it. It sat on my shelf in a special spot, that's how important it was to me. Books were rare, especially one of that quality. Mine was hardbound, just like the rows of books in the classroom in Davis, but not as thick. My dictionary, too, had colored pictures. As a girl, I had pored over its contents, tried to decipher the English words, and admired the wonderful illustrations.

The lack of textbooks and other reference books in Cambodia was, of course, one reason students there learned by rote. We, the hungry recipients, depended wholly on the teacher to feed us information. We respected and feared him as the source of knowledge, the giver or withholder of important facts. We could not turn to a nearby book for answers. Yet in Davis, with precious books readily available, the barefooted boy treated them like trash paper, and no one objected. I was outraged.

Mr. Livingston walked into the room in the middle of my reflections. Students greeted him with easy banter. He joked back with them. This was new to me also, but I liked it. These kids weren't afraid of their teacher.

Most students in my classes had failed to complete the requirements during the regular school year. Few were highly motivated. They came to class simply to get the needed credit. A school where students weren't eager to learn was another new and unsettling experience for me. School was neither free nor mandatory in Cambodia, so those who went valued it. It was a privilege few could afford.

I felt completely out of place in an American high school; the program wasn't geared to my level, but it fascinated me. What a window on popular culture. I felt like an anthropologist doing field work on an exotic tribe.

I found the subject matter in American History and in Social Studies amazing, the information entirely new to me. I resented the students for not paying better attention. I wanted to shake them for wasting an opportunity to learn. I could hardly wait for each class to begin; they just waited for it to end. I envied their ability to understand. I wished it were mine; after all, they weren't using it. It was frustrating to comprehend only half the material. I wanted it all. I longed for the ability to ask questions and have the teacher understand what I said without effort.

Early in the term, the class discussed World War II and the Nazi party. Before coming to America, I'd heard about Hitler, the bad guy. But I didn't know about the mass killings. My brother-in-law Ken had told me that lots of Jews had been killed, but it wasn't real to me. I couldn't picture it when I was a student in Phnom Penh any more than these secure, carefree, American students could. However, after what I'd lived through under the Khmer Rouge, I found the Nazis all too real.

Each week we watched a movie. With the door closed, the blinds pulled, and the lights out, the first film we saw was about Hitler and his Nazi followers. It showed mass graves of the Jewish people, gas chambers, mounds of bodies. Half way through the film I fled the room, gasping for air; I found it too similar to what I had recently experienced. I've since read *The Diary of Anne Frank* and now realize why teachers have called the first book about me the *Cambodian Diary of Anne Frank*. We had a lot in common, Anne and I, but I was lucky enough to survive. Her story is so powerful!

One week the movie covered black slavery. The kids thought I was weird because I cried all the way through the film. It was so heavy. I felt such empathy for the plight of the slaves. I knew firsthand the hopelessness they felt.

Another week we watched *Cover Girl*, a fascinating, light-hearted musical. At the end of the movie the teacher asked, "So, what year or years was it set in?" The kids all seemed to know. I sat in amazement. How had they figured it out? What had I missed? "What made you settle on that?" the teacher continued. Their answers were a revelation to me. "The style of the cars." "The clothes." "The kitchen appliances." My admiration for them grew. It had never occurred to me to pay attention to details, to analyze what I saw. I'd been taught to absorb and regurgitate, not analyze, contrast, and compare.

Mr. Livingston found me fascinating. He always asked me questions, but I had a hard time answering. One day the students were supposed to write an essay. I went to him fearfully and said, "I can't." "Don't worry, Teeda. It's okay." He was always so nice to me. I liked the other teacher too, but I can't remember his name; maybe it was Mr. Lee. The students, all white kids, were kind to me as well, but they didn't know what to make of me any more than I knew what to make of them.

One unit of study covered the war in Vietnam. That unit was extremely valuable to me. I began to understand what had happened to my country and why the spill-over fighting from Vietnam had embroiled Cambodia in that war also. The facts we learned in class were well documented; I especially appreciated that. Like other Cambodians, I did not really understand the background of what had happened in our country or to me personally, until I got to America. That unit on Vietnam and, later, the biography about my family filled huge gaps in my understanding.

I learned a lot from those two summer courses. I was only one or two years older than some kids, but we were worlds apart. I was old beyond my years in life experiences, but a baby compared to those students in knowing how to function in America. I could never have made it through a regular high school program with my limited English, and I would always have been upset at the kids' ingratitude and nonsense. But I learned as much from them as I did from the teachers and the course material. I treasure that first summer in America as a rare opportunity to have sampled a teenage world I'd never known. It will make me a better, more understanding mother when my own children are that age.

22 DELAYED CONFESSION

Vitou:

I-80 is no place to have car trouble, especially not The Causeway - that narrow neck of elevated freeway over the Sacramento River's flood plain. Yet there I was, an inexperienced driver trying to prove his manhood to a car-full of females.

My wife, Teeda, and I were living with the Criddles, one of our sponsoring families, at the time I borrowed their ancient Chevy Impala. I'd been in America for four months by then and had just passed my driver's test. Eager to show off my newly acquired skill, I took Teeda, two of her sisters, and her mother to nearby Sacramento to shop. Of course my nephew and five nieces went along. For them a car ride was still a novelty.

We were enjoying our drive immensely when we noticed a highway patrol car approaching from behind. "Duck," I yelled at the six kids. Once before our family had been caught with too many passengers in the car; we didn't want that to happen again.

Unfortunately, the air was oppressive near the floor; within minutes the children claimed, one after the other, that they needed to throw up. "Don't you dare!" their mothers threatened between bursts of laughter. "Not in a borrowed car." The patrolman gained on us so slowly I thought he'd never pass, but at last the ordeal was over. The kids came up for air, their high spirits restored by the time we reached the shopping mall.

We always had a good time shopping in America. Every trip was an adventure that revealed something different about our new homeland. After years of Khmer Rouge deprivation, we reveled in the abundance, even if we couldn't afford most of it.

Nervously but successfully I'd negotiated the big city traffic, and at last we were on our way home. Quite proud of my driving ability, I was about to congratulate myself aloud when the Chevy began to cough. As we coasted to a stop, I had no option but to pull onto the almost non-existent shoulder of the elevated freeway and try to figure out what was wrong.

More than the inconvenience of dealing with car trouble on a blistering July day in California's Central Valley, I worried that the Criddles might not trust me with their vehicle again. I'd hate that; like many a young man, I felt that being behind the wheel of a car was an extension of my still insecure manhood.

I'd grown up in Cambodia and, at just the age when I might have had a chance to drive, the Khmer Rouge enslaved us. For the next four years I planted and harvested rice; shinnied up sugar palms to collect sap; hunted wild game in the jungle; and listened to mind-numbing harangues on why we should willingly sacrifice our lives for the good of the utopian society they claimed to be building with a nations' sweat and blood. Stuck in a thatch-roofed village in the back of beyond, I seldom saw a vehicle, let alone got my hands on one. So, as an almost twenty-two-year-old who'd missed this rite of passage, sitting behind the wheel of a huge American car was my idea of manhood made manifest. I didn't want to be denied wheels even if they were on a borrowed 1968 Impala.

As the youngest of the sons-in-law, I was still trying to establish myself as a man in the eyes of my wife's family. Being twenty years younger than Ken and Leng proved to be a distinct disadvantage in achieving that goal. I certainly did not relish, once again, revealing my inadequacies the first time I took the women for a drive. But there was no help for it. I tried to think what might cause a stall.

I hoped one day to be a mechanic, if not a full-fledged engineer, but to date I'd had more access to monkeys than to monkey wrenches, let alone cars. Fortunately, this time I was in luck. It did not take long to discover that we'd only run out of gas.

Well, at least I could handle that, I told myself. Then I realized I might not have enough command of English to make myself understood. Sheepishly I asked Teeda to walk down the freeway with me to a gas station; her English was better than mine. Pooling everyone's money, we found we had only $5.78. Oh well, enough to get home, I thought.

Unfortunately, the young service station attendant thought otherwise. In response to our uncomprehending stares, the frustrated attendant gave what I suppose was an explanation. Teeda and I consulted and finally guessed he wanted a $10 deposit on the gas can. We'd never heard of such a thing.

Now this was a dilemma. Either I could offer him our $5.78 as a deposit on the can, or I could buy gas but not both. With gestures and broken English we tried to explain the problem. Shrugging, he moved off to help another attendant wait on customers.

When he returned, I was searching my pockets for something of value. Nothing. In desperation I took off my sweat-stained shirt to offer as collateral. By the dumbfounded look on his face we knew he finally understood the problem. His refusal was just as evident.

Then to our great relief he smiled, took our money, filled the gas can, and motioned us toward his truck. Still unwilling to trust us with his container - or perhaps just sorry for the poor immigrants having to hoof it down the hot asphalt - he gave us a ride back to the stalled Chevy and our now anxious relatives. He even poured the gas into our tank, smiling and trying to joke with the children as he did. We could only nod, return the smile, and repeat "Thank you, thank you," as he hopped in his truck, waved to the kids, then sped down the freeway.

Americans really are amazingly generous people, we told ourselves, not for the first time since we'd come to this land of opportunity. However, not wanting to press my luck or prejudice the Criddles against loaning me their car again, I didn't get around to mentioning this incident to them for eleven years.

23 MATH AND OTHER IMPORTANT MATTERS
By Shirley Jones

The sight of a student sitting with Ted at the kitchen table was no novelty in our house by the time Vitou took his place as the latest to be tutored. By then, my son had taught math to students of all ages and stages, from junior high through college. He'd never had a student like Vitou, though.

For one thing, Vitou started from scratch in a way no Davis student ever did. Deprived of educational opportunities at a young age, he had little to build on. What he had learned in school had been mostly lost during his years under the Khmer Rouge, when just surviving had taken all his energy and ingenuity. In addition, Vitou came to America with no knowledge of western languages to help him bridge the gap from Cambodian to English.

But if the barriers facing him were formidable, his determination was more than a match for them. By the time he arrived at our house each afternoon at 1:00, he had already bicycled to the neighboring town of Woodland to attend four hours of adult school, then cycled back in the fierce heat of summer's midday in California's central valley. He never missed a session. He worked hard every minute he was with Ted, struggling to learn the concepts he needed to pass the GED exams and earn the all-important high school equivalency certificate, his *open sesame* to higher education in California.

The hour he spent in our home was just one small piece of the jigsaw puzzle that was Vitou's life that summer. After leaving us, he worked for four hours, where he pumped gas and learned simple car repair. At night he studied to prepare for the next day's lessons. Always he struggled to improve his comprehension of English.

Vitou placed a high value on the time he spent with Ted. If unable to get to the session on time, he always called. He thanked Ted when each session ended, and often he brought us such gifts as he was able to obtain, especially fish he caught in the local creek. When did he find time to catch fish? We couldn't imagine!

At the same time that he was learning the educational basics at school and with his tutor, Vitou was also learning a lot about American culture, behavior, and speech patterns. Sometimes trying to fit his own values into the new culture presented special difficulties.

For instance, courtesy was a basic component of his cultural heritage, and he was anxious to treat his sponsors and helpers with respect. However, he didn't yet have enough familiarity with English usage to know what form of address was appropriate and wouldn't risk giving offense by using the wrong one. As a result, he always used the entire name of whomever he referred to. When he spoke to me on the phone and Ted wasn't at home, he invariably referred to "Ted Jones" each time he used his name. One afternoon he told Ted about some experience he'd had with one of his sponsors and throughout the story called her "Mrs. Kathryn Gardner." Though he may not have been entirely comfortable in navigating the rapids of an unfamiliar language and culture, it was touching to see that the years of hardship and deprivation had not diminished Vitou's innate courtesy and gratitude.

During this period, Vitou and his wife, Teeda, attended a Halloween party which Ted remembers as an experience that presented a lot more confusion than enlightenment about their new country's customs. Although it was a costume party, that was about the only traditional aspect of the occasion. At one point someone had the great idea of writing new Halloween words to some Christmas carols. The group then visited a family in the neighborhood known for their flexibility and serenaded them with "Halloween carols."

A political discussion added to the general confusion. Ted and Vitou were talking about his experiences in Cambodia when a third young man joined the conversation. He was in the stage of life where political opinions are first being formed, in this case with little understanding to base them on. He had heard of the evils of socialism, and when he heard Vitou describe terrible conditions under which he had lived in his homeland he assured Vitou that this must have been due to socialism. Communism, he declared, had something going for it; he had read the *Manifesto* and could see that there were some good ideas there. But socialism was unadulterated evil. Throughout the conversation Vitou looked as though he were thinking, "This must make sense, if only I could understand it." And Ted was thinking, "This doesn't make any sense to me, much less to Vitou."

While Vitou learned math from Ted, we learned from him. Just as his time with Ted was important to him, it became increasingly valuable to us as well.

Eventually Vitou moved to the San Francisco Bay area and passed from our lives, but not before he passed the GED exams, went on to Sacramento City College and got a degree in airplane mechanics.

The time we spent with him opened our eyes to a greater understanding of the immigrant experience and Vitou's own variation on that theme. We could see, what at that time he could not, that this extraordinary young man had what it takes to gain his own version of the American dream.

24 DIVORCE PENDING

Vitou:

I married Teeda, a stranger, just four days before the Khmer Rouge regime fell unexpectedly in January 1979. Our reasons for marrying evaporated with their loss of control over our lives, but I'd learned to love Teeda during those few days and thought she felt the same toward me. So, unlike many we knew, we decided to stay married, at least for the time being.

Many couples, who married under the same forced arrangements, divorced. It wasn't a real divorce, they just quit living together. Since people didn't feel married, they felt no need to get a formal divorce. Because the Khmer Rouge imposed marriage on couples, it seemed fake, especially since it had none of the trappings Cambodians associate with a wedding: public commitments by both families, a long engagement, exchange of gifts, parties, promises to each other and vows of fidelity, hair-cutting ceremonies, special clothes, special jewelry and foods, Buddhist ceremonies. Without these to bind them, couples felt no shame in walking away from such marriages when it became possible.

My childhood in Cambodia contrasted sharply with Teeda's secure upbringing in a loving, stable, extended family. I came from a broken home, shunted from relative to relative who treated me, I felt, more like a servant than a son. I attributed my parents' escalating discord and ultimate divorce to our living near to too many maneuvering in-laws. Everyone seemed to mind our family's business but us.

As a young man, I'd decided never to marry, but, if I did, I vowed to do everything possible to keep the marriage together, especially if we had children. No child of mine would come from a broken home.

I pretty much raised myself and, by the time I married, had grown accustomed to making my own decisions. So, although I admired and envied the close relationship Teeda had with her family, I found it difficult to adjust not only to a stranger for a wife, but to the constant presence of my wife's relatives as well.

All of us lived together day and night for over a year, first, as we tried to escape from Cambodia, then in the crowded Thai refugee camps. There was little privacy, and decisions were made by the group, especially by the older members of the family. I often felt odd man out.

By the time we reached America, Teeda's relatives had even begun planning my life and suggesting careers. They seemed to expect too much of me, forgetting that while the men in her family had enjoyed prestigious, established careers before the Khmer Rouge came to power, I'd been just a kid in Phnom Penh.

As the youngest son-in-law and the only one not related by blood, my opinions didn't seem to count. I felt my wife's loyalties remained with her mother and sisters instead of shifting to me. And she seemed to take advice from her oldest brother-in-law, Ken, as head of the extended family, without consulting me. Begrudgingly, I admitted he often had better ideas, but that seemed beside the point.

So, when my young bride and I arrived in America, I wanted to cement our relationship away from her extended family. However, that was not immediately possible, because we'd all been sponsored to the same small community by the same people. I sometimes envied Samol for having Teeda's sister Soorsdey to himself in Canada.

Then, two months after we came to America, the adult school

that Teeda and I attended closed for the summer. This seemed a logical time to move elsewhere or, at least, to check out the possibility. Besides, I longed to see more of America than the sleepy little university community of Davis. It felt lonely being the only Cambodians in town. I wanted us to visit my aunt in Los Angeles and my brother in Washington D.C. and to look over those cities as possible places to settle. Teeda would have none of it. She liked arrangements just as they were.

I tried forcing the issue. She remained adamant, countering that Ken and her mother didn't like the idea. She pointed out that we had supportive sponsors and lived in a fine community. We were lucky; I should be content.

In true Cambodian macho fashion, I attempted to assert my position as her husband, assuming I had the right, by time-honored custom, to order her to do as I said. I over-played my hand by saying she was no wife of mine if she would not come with me. I wanted to prove her love with an ultimatum. This put me in an awful trap. I bought round trip bus tickets to Washington D.C. by way of Los Angeles.

When Teeda drove me to the station in Sacramento, I kept hoping she would let me save face by convincing me to stay or by coming with me. Although she acted friendly, she let me board the bus and leave. I felt betrayed. It seemed she'd again shown where her loyalties really rested, just as she had on one of our escape attempts from Cambodia when the family left Leng and me behind.

On that former occasion, we all waited in the border town of Poipet for a chance to escape to Thailand. We needed all the financial assets we could get, so the family trusted Leng and me with our oxen, cart, and other bulky valuables. We planned to sell them in a city a day's journey inland. Relatively safe times to cross into Thailand came only occasionally, so I made Teeda promise to leave with her family if such an opportunity came before Leng and I got back from Sisophon. When the two of us returned to the family hut in Poipet, just three and a half days later, they were gone! Apparently we were both expendable.

Teeda's explanations when we next met seemed logical, but the feeling of being marginal to her lingered, and still surfaces whenever we quarrel. I certainly felt marginal on that bus ride to Los Angeles. I knew she'd married me out of desperation not love. She claimed that had changed, but being left behind when she and her family escaped Cambodia seemed to prove otherwise. Now, when I wanted her to follow me, she'd chosen to stay in Davis with her family. She claims my sense of rejection as a child left me insecure and colors our relationship. She's probably right, but . . .

Desperate with love for her, I called from Los Angeles. She wouldn't talk to me. In her mind I'd divorced her; she claimed nothing more needed discussing. I talked to Ken hoping he'd defend me to Teeda. He was really angry with me for leaving. He put it graphically with a Cambodian analogy: If you collected the finest rice from throughout the world, you'd not find a grain as precious as the one you've just discarded. I knew he was right, but I hadn't discarded her, she'd discarded me! He continued berating me, putting down my abilities and reminding me of all my shortcomings: a quick temper, impetuousness, lack of English proficiency, little education, inability to earn a good living in America. . . .

Wow! I felt totally rejected. So hurt. With Teeda's relatives as a majority on one side, I stood alone not knowing where to turn. I had no advocate. I'd never meant our little tiff to explode into a major event or to involve her whole family. I could understand Teeda getting angry; in many ways I'd married a young girl who'd never grown up much, and I'd handled the disagreement poorly. She looked to Ken as her mentor; I had a hard time measuring up to an educated man twice my age.

I understood that in her anger she might say things she didn't really mean, just as I had, but I'd not anticipated the family siding with her. All the things I'd done for them and with them during the past year seemed to count for nothing. I didn't know how to respond or what to try next. I didn't know about marriage counselors then, but if I had, I might even have turned to one despite the loss of face that would mean from an Asian male's perspective.

By the time I'd been in Los Angeles a week, I realized it would be almost impossible for me to earn enough there to save any money. It was no place to get ahead. And though it felt good to be around lots of Cambodians, I saw for the first time the disadvantages. They'd formed a ghetto, a little Phnom Penh. Many who'd been in America for years couldn't speak English as well as I could after just a couple of months.

Teeda continued to hang up whenever I called, so I decided to go on to Washington D.C. to see my brother. I still had the bus ticket, and I needed more time to decide what to do.

It felt great to see my brother again, but Washington offered no more than Los Angeles had. Besides, my brother and his wife were having troubles of their own, and not long after my visit they divorced. As with so many other refugees, the strain of adjusting to a new country and culture proved more than their marriage could sustain. I didn't want to lose Teeda, but what could I do if she would not let me return, wouldn't even speak to me?

My marriage seemed lost, but I refused to give up without trying. One of my traits that Ken identified as stubbornness, I preferred to call tenacity. So although I felt the family had closed ranks and would not accept me under any terms, I had to make the effort. I refused to fail by default. I'd made a serious mistake by leaving; if they kicked me out when I returned, maybe that would be their mistake too. I couldn't know unless I confronted them in person.

I felt terrible on the bus ride back to California. I still didn't know what to do. I didn't have a plan. I kept saying, "I'm a man. I'm free to go, but at least I will have tried." That long ride gave me too much time for reflection. My spirits fell even lower when my thoughts harked back to other proofs that I could never be what Teeda wanted of me. Before we escaped from Cambodia, I'd come across her old diary and read her description of the kind of man she hoped to marry - older, educated . . . , all the things I was not. Wow, I thought, I'm not her type. She had laughed it off at the time, saying she wrote that before she fell in love with me.

One other memory from that escape time haunted me on the bus ride. As we had struggled westward on Cambodia's crowded roads, I met people who had known Teeda's family in Phnom Penh years before. They prophesied that when Teeda's family no longer needed my assistance in escape, they'd dump me; I didn't come from the same social strata. I refused to believe them. The joy Teeda and I found in each other's company and her family's warm acceptance of me belied that assertion. Now I wondered. That cross-continent bus trip did nothing to boost my confidence as I neared California and my fate.

When the bus stopped in Salt Lake City, a long day's ride from Sacramento, I called Louise Kenner, one of our sponsors. It seemed my only hope. I felt sure Teeda's family would not accept me without help. I asked Louise if she would talk to Ken and the others before I arrived the next day. I hoped she could convince Teeda to at least let me speak to her. It seemed unfair to turn me away without even a hearing.

Until I called, my sponsors knew only that I'd gone to visit my aunt and my brother. They knew nothing of our marital problems or my agony. Louise agreed to meet the bus in Sacramento and to see what else she could do.

Only later did I learn what happened in Davis while I rode west. Louise consulted with our other sponsors. All of them felt ill prepared to intervene. They had no way of knowing if I even deserved a hearing, or if we'd be better off together or going our separate ways. But if the family would not let me return, my sponsors felt responsible for finding another place for me to live. The Criddles agreed I could stay with them but wanted to be sure that Teeda and her relatives understood that this did not imply they were taking sides.

Louise Kenner and Dick Criddle dreaded butting into our family's affairs but mustered the courage to talk to Ken. Ken said the decision must be Teeda's alone. The others would back whatever she wanted. Surprisingly, most didn't even know the nature or the seriousness of our disagreement. Ken and Teeda's mother had kept that to themselves.

Joan Criddle then talked to Teeda and learned she felt as hurt and rejected as I did, but still cared deeply. However, she assumed it was already too late; I'd divorced her. When Joan assured her that was not the case, either by my intent or in the legal sense, Teeda finally agreed to talk with me. But she was not ready to have me return to the apartment before we'd seen if our differences were reconcilable.

Teeda felt unsure of trusting her future to someone so different from her calm, careful, mature brothers-in-law. By nature, Ken and Leng were cautious men, something I never had been or likely would be.

Teeda wanted some evidence that I would never walk out on her again, that I'd settle down, continue my education, and show some ability to earn a living, that I would be part of the extended family and accept them as she felt they accepted me.

I ached to be with my wife but moved in with the Criddles, determined to prove I was trustworthy and steady. Willingly, I would have promised to be or do anything Teeda asked, if she would just take me back. Joan counseled me to make no such promises. She said, "I know you mean it now, and you would sincerely try to keep those promises, but in the long run you simply could not. Besides, Teeda wouldn't want such a wimp. She is a strong young woman and wants a strong husband she can rely on, not rule."

Joan suggested ways to show Teeda she could put her trust in me. I enrolled in summer school classes in a nearby city and biked there daily. I got part-time work in a service station and auto body shop. I met with Ted Jones, a fellow my age, who helped me with math so I could pass the high school equivalency exams. Joan advised that I continue with these activities for several weeks before approaching Teeda to plead my case. Well, that was one piece of advice I couldn't follow. Impatience must be my second name; as soon as I'd signed up for the classes, I biked to our apartment hoping I'd proved my good intentions. That is just what Teeda thought they were, good intentions. She expected evidence of my follow-through before resuming our relationship.

I returned to the Criddles with such a hangdog expression that Joan could hardly stand it. She again counselled keeping my distance. Teeda told her that she felt pressured, she needed time to think. I tried to give her that, but somehow my bike just kept taking me to the apartment each afternoon to see if enough time had passed yet. I felt so love-sick and forlorn I could hardly concentrate on my studies. I developed shingles, which made my physical pain almost a match for my emotional torment.

Some very important things happened in our relationship that long, long summer. We courted. We spent many hours talking about things of importance. We learned to be very honest with each other about our feelings - something alien to Cambodian culture, which encouraged hiding and denying inner turmoil.

Although technically still married, we used this opportunity to decide if marriage to one another was really what each of us wanted. Under the Khmer Rouge, others had made our marriage decision. This time, if we resumed our marriage, it needed to be on our own terms. It would be our choice, not someone else's - what an awesome responsibility. We had no culturally appropriate pattern to fall back on and felt like pioneers charting unknown territory.

We watched the Criddles' teenaged daughters, Pam and Karen, date and saw value in the American system of getting to know a person before committing your life to them. But even after we'd recommitted to each other, there was the awkwardness of my rejoining the family circle. Just when and how should that happen?

Previously, arrangements had been made for the extended family to move into the Criddle home in mid-August when they left the country for eighteen months. Teeda finally agreed that when the family moved in I could stay, and we could again begin living as husband and wife. Realizing we would find it less awkward, and that we really needed time to ourselves, Joan convinced Teeda to move in a month early and help run the house when she left to be present for the birth of her first grandchild. So, at last Teeda and I were alone together - with Dick, Pam, and two Japanese exchange students!

Looking back from the vantage point of twelve years, I realize our marital crisis turned out to be a good thing, despite the anguish it caused us. We learned early in our marriage that before taking serious steps you need to talk deep and long. You must learn to articulate how you feel and listen with your heart to what the other person says. We'd imputed motives to each other that weren't correct. We'd been distrustful and suspicious. We'd allowed the fact that we'd not made the original decision to marry be an excuse for not working at it hard enough.

I learned that ultimatums don't work. Refusing to talk about differences doesn't work, and trying to follow one culture's ways of handling a problem, when living in another culture, without modification is deadly. I'd been so concerned about *losing face* that I nearly lost a wife.

In Cambodia I knew men who commanded a lot of power and control in their marriages; I tried it. It didn't work. It took something as traumatic as our impending divorce to wake me up, to make me realize that I didn't even want that kind of relationship. I've become part of a new generation of Cambodian-American men who don't want control. We no longer equate power over wife and children with proof of manhood. We want a partner and friend for a wife.

I've also seen that men who refuse to adjust to the new freedoms that immigrant women expect here, only hurt themselves. Like bamboo, both the husband and the wife must bend, or their relationship will break. Gaining that flexibility has not been easy, but it has been worth it.

25 AN HONEST DAY'S WORK
By Dennis Huntington

An honest day's work for an honest day's pay is an old cliche most of us have heard, but, unfortunately, many do not live by. Vitou Mam was a young man who practiced this adage.

Vitou first worked for me pumping gas at my service station. He was anxious to do a good job, but because of his very limited command of the English language, he had a hard time communicating with customers. I thought it might work out better to move him over to my auto body shop. I worried about this as he had almost no knowledge of auto mechanics. He didn't even know the English names of the tools we used or the names of the car parts.

It would be hard to teach him without being able to communicate effectively. There could easily be misunderstandings. Even when we know a language, it's sometimes hard to communicate feelings. One would think these handicaps would make him an almost useless employee. This was definitely not the case.

The following characteristics are those most desired in an employee, according to a nationwide survey of employers:

honesty, punctuality, dependability, pride in work, respect for authority, and getting along with others. Vitou already knew and practiced all these. In a world market where worker theft, tardiness, and lack of motivation are occurring at an alarming rate, being able to trust an employee is very important to me. Of course, in my business, experience and skill are important also, but I could tell from the beginning that this would not hinder Vitou.

He watched, listened, and learned. His mind was like a computer, processing all that he saw and heard. He was eager to gain new knowledge. When I answered a question of his, he spent some time thinking about it. Then if he didn't understand, he asked again. He watched mechanics do a certain job, then he tried it. Usually he did it correctly. In asking questions, Vitou was very considerate and tried never to be in the way or slow down a mechanic. He understood that the mechanic had given the customer an estimate of how long a particular job would take and how much it would cost.

I had Vitou work closely with Mike, one of my best mechanics. I soon wondered if this had been a mistake. Mike is not a people person. He had gone through some really hard times. His baby was born paralyzed from the waist down. He had lost his twenty-three-year-old wife to cancer. He had had some terrible experiences in Vietnam.

Although Vitou was Cambodian, not Vietnamese, Mike was hard on him. I worried how Vitou could let some of the things Mike said just roll off his back, but when I learned of Vitou's background, I realized that nothing could be as bad as what he had already gone through. He and Teeda, his wife, looked like an ideal, happy, young couple without past trauma. It was hard to keep in mind the awful things they had endured. It wasn't long before Vitou won Mike over, and they developed a close relationship.

I obtained an old car for Vitou that needed work done on it.

Vitou was busy working, going to school, and studying, but he spent his lunch hour and any spare time working on that car. He wanted to do as much as he could by himself, so the other mechanics and I stood by giving advice and occasionally some help. There was a dent in his car, and just by watching what the other workers did, he was able to hammer out, sand, and paint the dent without help. I was amazed at how well he had done. It looked like a professional job.

After he got the car running, he and Teeda wanted to take a trip to Los Angeles. I worried all weekend, concerned that the old car might not make it, but Vitou came driving in Monday morning, right on time.

Vitou always kept busy doing whatever he could, no matter how menial the task. He cleaned engine parts and fetched tools. When there appeared to be nothing else to do, he still found something, even if it was only sweeping the floor.

It can be very boring doing the same things over and over. I knew he was anxious to do some *real* mechanical work. I'm sure he must have become discouraged at times, but he never complained. He seemed to have set a goal of learning something new each day.

One day, I took Vitou with me in my small airplane to pick up some parts in Lincoln, California. When we were airborne, I let him take the controls. It was then that I learned of his dream to work on airplanes. Several years later, I was pleased to find out he had realized his dream. I knew he could do it.

Vitou knew the value of work, something many people never learn. Having the health and strength to work and being free to work at something one enjoys is indeed a great privilege and an opportunity. Vitou always gave an honest day's work for an honest day's pay.

26 GRANDMOTHER OF THE HILLS
By Mary Lowry

"Stand up. . . . Walk to the door. . . . Open the door. . . . Good!" We laughed and felt silly, this Cambodian matriarch and I. In the best tradition of reinforcing language learning through use of the senses and bodily movement, we were acting out the Total Physical Response Method.

Once a week we trudged around her house, picking up, pointing to, opening, sitting, standing. We also painstakingly printed the English alphabet on her grandchildren's wide-lined school paper. She was proud of every little triumph, a *C* that did not close like an *O*, letters that sat on the line, her name *Ean Bun*.

A week later she had always forgotten the past lesson. I struggled to find the key that would open her to my language, but, unlike her daughters, sons-in-law, and grandchildren, she surrounded herself with her own language. She scolded the children in Khmer, she cooked in Khmer, she greeted, offered food, and gave advice in Khmer. Although she answered the phone in English, she couldn't get beyond "Hello." Still, during our weekly sessions she lit up with smiles and made clear to me with her hands and her few English words that she enjoyed the time we spent. I was a contact and a caring presence and, most likely, a welcome break from the two toddlers she cared for.

She never could tell us directly what she had suffered. In Cambodia, she had been the wife of a member of the legislature and the mother of four graceful, intelligent, wide-smiling women. They lived in a large, white, balconied family house, which they

left in 1975, and never saw again. During their trek from Phnom
Penh to the rural part of Cambodia she had been separated
from her husband. His execution was never confirmed, but she
never saw him or heard news of him again. She showed me his
picture and, gesturing, reminded me of the violence of his death;
her anger and sorrow poured out in a stream of Khmer I could
not understand. The tears she wiped away quickly told me
enough. After years of forced labor in a communal farming
area, Grandmother had twice walked two hundred miles to cross
the border into Thailand. After the first crossing, she and her
family, along with tens of thousands of other Cambodians, had
been forced back over the border at gunpoint by the Thais into
land-mined mountains. The good fortune of one daughter and
her family to be sent to the United States at that time must have
seemed to Grandmother a great personal loss. It took nine
months more before thirteen members of this clan were reunited
in California.

She felt separation keenly. Though most of the extended
family lived in Davis, for a time all under one roof, she would
grow melancholy about the daughter whose resettlement had
taken her to Canada. One Thursday, after half-hearted attempts
at her English lesson, she sat with her head bowed and the white
handkerchief balled in her hand. "Soorsdey . . ." - a sweeping
gesture pointed toward Canada. "Mearadey . . ." - another
gesture to show this daughter, too, was leaving her for a time -
"San Jose!" Then a gesture of pain toward herself and her
heart. We sat and held each other for a few minutes. I felt
some sense of the repeated loss she suffered as I realized how
soon they all would leave our community in their search for
work, a permanent home, and a secure life.

"Grandmother of the Hills" she calls herself now in Khmer.
Three daughters, each with children, have bought homes where
the edges of San Jose meet the hills. She travels from one to

the other as they need help. Her friends are Cambodian ladies who don't speak English either. She has no teacher there, she says. Brown and bare-footed in her draped and folded Cambodian skirt, she wears well the part of the matriarch of a sturdy survival.

27 AN UNWANTED PREGNANCY

Teeda:

I fled the Khmer Rouge nightmare and thought I'd shed its hated philosophies. They'd told us repeatedly - most often through slogans - that life was cheap, that to keep it was no benefit and to destroy it was no loss. That an individual's life could be compared to a single grain of rice, indistinguishable from any other grain and totally insignificant in itself.

My soul rebelled at such heresy when the Khmer Rouge applied this diabolical philosophy to me and my fellow countrymen. Yet, until six years ago, I never applied it to my own disregard for the welfare of an unborn child, my child.

I feel such remorse every time I think about the abortion I had in 1981, my second year in America. I feel especially sad about Kathryn, one of my sponsors, because, without knowing it, I'd asked her to do something she considered morally reprehensible. Yet her love for me would not allow her refuse to help me or to force her morality on me; although she knew I would have done anything she asked.

For four years, life for Cambodians had been reduced to bare essentials. It improved only slightly in 1979, the year I escaped my homeland and lived in squalid refugee camps in Thailand. All around me, women thought nothing of eliminating an unwanted pregnancy. We lived at the edge of endurance; one more stress might push any one of us into the abyss. Few felt they could afford the luxury of taking on an additional responsibility or a further drain on their energy.

By the time I'd been in America a year, life was not that bleak. Nonetheless, my husband and I were still recovering from those nightmarish years and trying to cope with our new surroundings. We had decided to wait to have children until we learned the language, gained job skills, and established ourselves in the work force.

Our sponsors had understood our desire to avoid pregnancy. So, shortly after I got to America, Joan and her married daughter Linda accompanied my sisters and me to the Davis Free Clinic for instruction on birth control options. I'd grown up in a culture that doesn't discuss private or personal matters. And I was more prudish than most Cambodian women when it came to talking about *that*, by which I meant anything to do with sex or reproduction. I even felt uncomfortable having my sisters in the same birth control session. However, I depended on Mearadey to translate. Also, she and Rasmei needed the same information about birth control options in America.

Linda, who is about my age, felt even more awkward than I did at the clinic. She was conspicuously pregnant with her first child, a planned for, hoped for event. We laughed that the instructor might think it odd for her to attend a birth control session when it was obviously too late.

The instructor used charts and diagrams to discuss reproduction and various birth control methods. Then Joan and Linda explained it to Mearadey in simpler words. Mearadey, in turn, re-explained the information to Rasmei and me in Cambodian. Fortunately, in Phnom Penh before our years under the Khmer Rouge, we'd had access to modern medical practices, so my two sisters, already married then, were aware of birth control methods. Otherwise, I don't know how much I would have understood from that three-layered discussion at the Davis clinic; the information was entirely new to me.

A year later, through carelessness, I became pregnant and

asked Kathryn if she would drive me to the doctor; I needed an abortion. At the time, I attached no more importance to the request than I did when asking her to drive me to the grocery store or the dentist.

Kathryn picked me up extra early and drove to a quiet spot. She parked the car, then solemnly turned to me, "Are you sure you want an abortion?" The question startled me. I thought, "Why is she asking me this?" Instead of considering, as I would now, if my decision was right or wrong, wise or unwise, I focused on trying to guess what she wanted me to say. I wondered if it would please her if I said I didn't want one. Did she think I shouldn't be doing this? If so, why? I tried to figure out what the socially correct answer might be, what Kathryn expected me to do. I loved and trusted our sponsor enough to do whatever she asked and was that inexperienced in making my own decisions.

I hesitated a moment while all this raced through my mind, then answered, "Ya." I suspect, now, that she misinterpreted the pause as an indication of deep consideration on my part. She merely replied in a subdued voice, "Okay, if you are sure." I again said, "Ya," to which she nodded and drove to the clinic.

I hadn't a clue what Kathryn tried to warn me about, but I sensed that it should have been important to me. That conversation and its setting stuck in my mind; I can still remember exactly where we parked, what she said, and the serious tone of her voice. Without my knowing the importance of the decision I was making, she had conveyed to me that it was, for some reason, an important decision, nonetheless.

Almost four years later, when Vitou and I were ready to start a family, I visited a relative in Stockton; she'd been pregnant at the time I had the abortion. Unlike my previous visits to her, this time when I saw her four-year-old daughter, it hit me like a physical blow; I'd aborted what otherwise would have been a child this age. I felt awful. At last, I understood the importance

Kathryn had attached to my decision. She wanted to be sure I'd considered the consequences, which I had not. She tried to prepare me for the possibility that someday I might regret my decision or feel guilty. Now, every time I see that little girl, I feel so sad, because I got rid of something that could have been a beautiful human being.

Even before my daughter was born, but especially after, I've thought about how much I love her. I have often asked myself, "Why didn't I value that beginning of a child like I value Laura?" I don't really blame myself; I was young and inexperienced. I had no background on which to base a wise judgment, and I was concerned with more immediate goals and needs.

Even more recently, I became aware of the personal sacrifice Kathryn made by taking me to the clinic. That realization came while watching a television show on abortion. For the first time, I listened carefully to the impassioned plea of a Pro-Life woman. Suddenly, I knew how Kathryn must have felt when I put her in such a moral dilemma. I'd had no idea what it meant to her. Now that I see how beautiful children are and know more about Kathryn's philosophy of life, I can appreciate how difficult it was for her to accompany me to do something she believed was so wrong.

I'm now the proud mother of two beautiful children. Laura Tevary and Andrew Tevuth are the joy of my life. I could never think of deliberately harming them, especially not destroying them. Yet that is what I did to the first child I conceived. I don't know what decision I'd have come to in '81 if I'd weighed all factors, but I deeply regret having acted without heartfelt consideration and full knowledge of the import of my decision. Again, I can only plead innocence regarding the seriousness of my act and wish it had been otherwise.

28 COLLEGE

Teeda:

People act surprised when they find out I earned an associate degree just three years after coming to America, especially when they learn that I arrived with less than a ninth grade education and didn't understand English. But they cannot be any more surprised than I was. For most of those three years I felt as though I moved in a fog, never really knowing what came next, where I was headed, or how to get there. I concentrated on the immediate task ahead and seemed to bump along in a zigzag pattern, trusting in teachers, counselors, family, sponsors, and friends to aim me this direction or that.

Due to cultural and language barriers, my sponsors thought I had more concrete goals - and plans for achieving them - than I actually did. They talked with me shortly after I arrived to find out what my career goals were so they could counsel me on how to reach them. Words such as *career, plan,* and *goals* were concepts almost beyond my imagination. My focus was much more immediate. I knew I must learn English and find a way to earn a living. Beyond that I didn't know what to expect. The cultural differences were too vast and my knowledge of the options open to me too narrow.

To help me, my sponsors asked what I, as a kid in prewar Cambodia, had wanted to be when I grew up. I've always been sure of one thing, I wanted education. I love learning. Among the things I resent most about my years under the Khmer Rouge were the years of school they stole from me.

In traditional Cambodia, few women worked outside the home, but adventurous girls of my generation dared consider advanced education or outside employment as a glamorous option. I'd thought about being a stewardess, a nurse, or a teacher. I had even dared hope I might be lucky enough to work for the prestigious American Embassy or another embassy in Phnom Penh, at least until I married. Those dreams died when I was fifteen, the year the Khmer Rouge won the civil war.

My sponsors decided that the first thing this almost twenty-year-old needed was a high school level education. So, even before my feet felt firmly planted in America, they had enrolled me in English courses and a high school continuation program.

In goal-oriented America, people often asked what I did. Glad to have a ready answer, I said proudly, "I'm a student at Fremont." That worked well until I was about to finish the high school equivalency program a year later. Then what? I really didn't know what came next.

Fortunately for me, I was with some Vietnamese classmates when they drove past Sacramento City College. I asked what those buildings and beautiful grounds were. They explained, then said I could go to school there, a prospect that excited me. I thought college was for rich people. We parked and they showed me around the campus.

One classmate said, "Not only can you go to school here, your expenses can be paid; they have scholarships for minority and low income students." I was amazed; imagine a country that made such wonderful opportunities available to disadvantaged kids. "You can even earn spending money," they continued. "I can? Great! How?" If accepted into the school, they said, I could talk to a guy in the financial aid center about help with tuition and books. Also, I could work on campus part time. It sounded like a fairy tale, with me as Cinderella (only I didn't know about her then).

I bought a catalog that listed majors and course requirements. Until then, I hadn't known so many subjects existed. Like a child let loose in a toy shop, I wanted some of everything. "How do I choose what classes to take? How do I sign up?" I wanted to know. The Vietnamese kids took me to the registration office.

"I want to go to school. What do I need to do?" The woman at the desk saw I was totally ignorant of where or how to begin.

She made an appointment for me with a school counselor for later in the week.

That night my husband and I pored over the various majors. He became excited too. He didn't get past the *As* before he'd found his major, Aeronautical Mechanics. I had less well defined interests.

When I met with the counselor, he asked, "How may I help you?" "Well," I hesitated, "I don't even know what questions to ask. I want to go to school." I said I wanted to be trained for a quiet job that allowed me to work by myself without the need to speak English - or as little as possible. (For the same reason, my sister Mearadey, thought the ideal job would be delivering mail.) Smiling at my naivete, this gentle, bearded, former hippy slowly and patiently took it from there. He explained that most jobs required some communication. Since I liked math, we narrowed my choices to accounting and computer programing. With surprise and relief, I learned that I didn't have to make a final decision on a career choice until after I'd sampled the first year courses. The counselor set me up with a beginning computer course, an accounting course, an English class, and a typing class.

Hours later, I left his office with a fairly clear idea of how to proceed. For the first time since coming to America, I caught a real glimpse of a future for me beyond school. And, I again had a pat answer for those ever curious, goal-oriented Americans.

I bought the text books and at home pored over the catalog again. I needed sixty-five credit hours to graduate in computer programing. I favored that major because it sounded important; my brother-in-law Ken, was taking computer science classes. Dividing the sixty five credits by four, I saw I'd need to take fifteen to eighteen credit hours each semester if I wanted to finish in two years. Unfortunately, Intermediate Algebra, a requirement in that major, had a prerequisite, Introduction to Algebra. Several other courses I needed for graduation also had prerequisites. I decided I didn't have time for those. Hoping to manage without the prerequisite courses, I looked through the intermediate algebra text book and decided I'd simply have to master the problems somehow and added that course to my other four.

At this point my husband and I told a sponsor we'd signed up for junior college. Kathryn's chin dropped. Apparently our sponsors saw college as a possibility in the future, but they didn't think we were ready yet. Our English was less than impressive. Kathryn sent Audrey Fowler, another sponsor, to school with us to find out what financial commitments we'd unwittingly made and to see if the counselor had any idea how little we knew. He said, "Oh, they'll do fine. We have lots of refugee students here." The financial aid office confirmed that they would pay for our tuition and books, but we had to successfully complete our first semester before applying for part-time work.

I had just stumbled upon this college opportunity. As far as I was concerned, a fortunate twist of fate made college students of us. However, I think our sponsors viewed it differently. They acted impressed with how goal-oriented we'd become and seemed surprised at how well Vitou and I had managed without their guidance. They admired our drive and ambition, unaware that we had almost no idea of what we'd let ourselves in for.

College took much more effort than we expected. The subject matter of the courses did not prove to be the stumbling block; it was the difficulty we still had with English. One teacher told Vitou, "You don't belong here. You need to go back and take more English."

I knew Vitou was becoming a real American when he told me he'd done a most un-Asian thing; he actually faced up to the teacher and explained that taking more English-as-a-Second-Language classes was not the answer. He could take ESL until doomsday and never learn the specialized language of aeronautical mechanics - they didn't cover those words. He said,

"If you need to, fail me. I'll just keep retaking the course until I understand and can pass, until I can read the text and understand what you are talking about." Vitou's logic made sense, so the teacher, somewhat taken aback but impressed with his pluck, agreed to let him try.

Unlike my major, Aeronautical Mechanics was a definite two year course that began only in September, with no opportunity to take it at a slower pace. If Vitou had taken time for remedial English, he would have had to wait a whole year before beginning his major. This put enormous pressure on him to succeed. His program based half the grade on written work and tests and the other half on lab projects. Vitou scored only 30% on his first test, but from there his scores went to 40%, to 50%, to 70% as his English improved. On his written assignments he usually got *D*s and *F*s, but on his lab projects he always got *A*s.

My experience in ESL classes at the adult school and at college left me with the same opinion Vitou had; after the first few levels, straight ESL didn't do much good. We'd found the classes boring and not relevant. Once we'd learned the basics of conversation - "Hello John." "Hi Mary." "How are you today?" "I am fine." "Nice weather isn't it." and so on - we needed language oriented to interesting subject matter that challenged us. We needed simple language spoken slowly that used words in context in a real school course. For instance, I'll never forget Mr. Tully's fascinating science course at Fremont. There I learned English while studying science. Another class that stands out in my mind is a college course called Business Philosophy. For me it opened a window onto Western thinking, a crash course on individualism and the American culture. I was surprised to learn that Americans focus on themselves and how they feel. They also analyze things, assuming everything has a logical answer. They are taught to analyze how something will affect them personally, then select a course of action and take responsibility for the consequences. Those were novel ideas to me.

This Business Philosophy class helped me look at a difficulty I'd had in my marriage in a new light. I'd grown up letting others make decisions for me, or I made decisions based on what I thought would please my adult relatives. When Vitou and I had a marital problem shortly after arriving in America, my concern had been what my relatives might want me to do, not what I wanted. This course made me realize that such problems were not for them to decide. Primarily it involved Vitou and me. We had to make our own decisions. More specifically, I had to make up my own mind about what I considered important. That course hit me at the right time; as a married woman, I must no longer function as a child. No longer would I let others be my primary decision makers. The idea of taking responsibility for decisions that affected me was a real eye opener and a challenge.

A marketing class taught me the economics of supply and demand. I learned practical information that gave me new insight into the business world and how to function better as a consumer in America. Almost everything I learned in my classes was new, exciting, useful information. Struggling over homework assignments and trying to understand all the unfamiliar English words in the texts seemed a small price to pay for the wealth of knowledge I gained.

After the first semester, I worked part time in the college library. It was great! I learned how to find information on any subject. That, too, is a gift I treasure. Until then, I didn't know how valuable libraries could be. Currently, I'm sampling the literature of the West by reading during my lunch hour and by listening to audio cassettes as I drive to and from work. I just finished *The Joy Luck Club*. Fantastic!

Junior college proved to be a heady experience, one I could have enjoyed for years, but reality impinged and kept me focused on graduating on schedule. I needed to earn a living. As a result, there are huge gaps in my knowledge. People I work with use terms from chemistry or biology as if they were everyday words. They learned that information in high school and are surprised when I don't know what they are talking about. I am very good at what I do in the field of computer programing, and I've learned to use English with a certain degree of sophistication; therefore, colleagues assume I've had a typical Western education. However, I've never had the privilege of a biology or chemistry course, a musical education or art lessons, a cooking class or sewing instruction. I've missed studying the literary heritage of the West - or of the East for that matter. There is so much I do not know, but I will be forever grateful to a group of Vietnamese students who opened the world to me when we went for a drive one day past Sacramento City College.

Recently, I told my sponsor Joan how lost I felt when I began school in America and how haphazardly I thought I had proceeded. She laughed. "Well, that may be so, but if you had set out with a firm goal and worked determinedly and single-mindedly to get your high school equivalency and graduate from junior college in record time, you could not have done it any faster." Surprised, I realized she was right.

29 CHRISTIANS AND BUDDHISTS

Ken and Mearadey Ngak had been in America four months when I met them in the fall of 1979. They and their three young daughters came to Davis, California under the sponsorship of the local Lutheran Church and shortly after arriving became members of that congregation.

Our group of five sponsoring families worked with Ken, Mearadey, and their Lutheran sponsors to bring Mearadey's relatives to California. During these efforts the Ngaks became better acquainted with us and learned that members of our group belonged to a different Christian denomination than their sponsors. I became vaguely aware that this seemed to cause Ken some concern.

Shortly before the arrival of Mearadey's family, Ken put his apprehension into words: "Do you expect our relatives to join the Mormon Church?"* We assured him that this was not a condition of our sponsorship. We explained carefully that we would enjoy sharing our beliefs, but religion is a very personal matter and something they must ultimately decide for themselves.

His quick reply surprised me. "Good, because we all want to belong to the same church." From that statement I assumed that, following his own family's conversion to the Lutheran faith, Ken and Mearadey had converted their relatives, perhaps through letters, during the five months Mearadey's extended family lived in the refugee camp in Thailand. Not long after her relatives arrived in mid-March 1980, I learned that they, too, had accepted Lutheran baptism. This reinforced my opinion that conversion must have taken place before they came to America.

A few months later, my family left for one and a half years abroad. Ken's family of five and their eight relatives moved into our house and settled more firmly into their new homeland.

While overseas, I researched the history of Indochina and wrote the biography of these remarkable Cambodian friends. This effort culminated a few years later in the book *TO DESTROY YOU IS NO LOSS: The Odyssey of a Cambodian Family.* Just before returning to America, I visited a Cambodian refugee camp in Thailand. I went to Khao-I-Dang, near the Thai-Cambodian border, specifically to observe the refugee experience firsthand. I wanted to be sure the details I'd written were correct before I approached a publisher about my book.

While touring the refugee camp, I picked up literature designed to help Westerners understand the Indochinese refugees

---

* This is a popular nickname for The Church of Jesus Christ of Latter-day Saints.

they sponsored - especially refugees from village or tribal back-grounds.[*] I found the literature interesting, but dismissed it as not particularly applicable to our friends because they'd been city people. The brochures recounted the Buddhist and animist beliefs of most Cambodians and mentioned Buddhism's ability to absorb many doctrines within its broad philosophy. The literature further advised Westerners not to be surprised if the refugees they sponsored joined the dominant religion in whichever community they settled; they wanted to fit in. A variation of that advice said that refugees might join their sponsor's church to show gratitude and respect. Only fleetingly did I wonder if our friends' conversion to Christianity had been genuine.

In March of 1982, I returned to Davis. By then, only Vitou and Teeda lived in our home. The other adults had completed their education and one by one found work in Silicon Valley.

As I dressed for church the first Sunday after my return, Vitou and Teeda left for their Lutheran worship service. I was impressed. This young couple had been on their own for months and were, apparently, participating in religious worship based on their own beliefs and not on family or outside pressure.

Later that day, I recounted highlights from the sermon I'd heard and asked about theirs. Teeda retrieved palm fronds from the trash and replied with a question in her voice, "Well, they gave us these." It took only a few questions to ascertain that she and Vitou made no connection between these fronds and religion, nor did they understand the significance of Palm Sunday. They did not know the next Sunday would be Easter. They knew almost nothing about Christ's death and resurrection or the profound significance these events have for Christians. I then realized they'd joined the Lutherans for the very reasons the literature described. Even so, I was surprised that they knew

---

[*] This literature was prepared by the United Nations High Commission For Refugees and by the French government.

so little about basic Christianity or specific Lutheran beliefs.

I said, "Teeda, surely the pastor and others talked to you about their beliefs before you were baptized? You must have had specific lessons about basic doctrine." She looked puzzled, then answered hesitatingly, "Well, maybe so. They did come to the house a few times and we met with the pastor for awhile. Maybe that was what they were doing. They talked about Jesus and other stuff. We didn't understand most of what they said. The words were too hard."

"Then why did you join?"

"Well, they are nice people. We like being with them. They offer friendship, have high standards, and my sisters liked the quality friends my nieces and nephew found there. We could practice English. Besides, Ken and Mearadey had already joined."

"But, that congregation would still have offered fellowship even if you hadn't joined."

"We didn't know that for sure and couldn't take the chance. We needed their friendship."

As we talked, it became evident that the pastor and others had been diligent in explaining their church's doctrines. Apparently, they thought Teeda's family understood the discussions, believed the message, and accepted the baptismal commitment. The fact that the entire family had gone to Sunday services routinely and joined in church related activities, no doubt, appeared as further evidence of their commitment.

Obviously, the gulf between the two cultures was so vast that neither group realized they were not bridging it - there was no common basis for religious communication. (Later I'm sure, many members of the congregation understood that the refugees' knowledge was limited and their commitment to Christianity tentative, but their friendship and sincerity were genuine.)

During our discussion, Teeda realized for the first time that she'd made commitments without real understanding. She felt both Lutheran and Buddhist and yet neither. She had not understood that she'd become a Christian just by having "a little water sprinkled" on her and joining in fellowship with the Lutherans. To her it was like joining the Campfire Girls, Rotary Club, or League of Women Voters - all organizations with worthwhile goals and high ideals but with no demand for exclusivity. Nor did she know that when Buddhists joined a Christian church they were automatically assumed to be renouncing Buddhism.

Except for Teeda's mother, who was devout but not knowledgeable about her beliefs, the family felt only nominally Buddhist. However, Teeda saw no need to renounce Buddhism and did not consider she had. It was as much a part of her as the air she breathed. She had thought she could be both, and many other things besides. She never understood that to most Westerners it was an either/or choice.

For the first fifteen years of her life, Teeda had not been actively Buddhist, and for the next four years religious practice was officially banned. Until Teeda came to America, she did not know other religions existed, not even other forms of Buddhism. Therefore, it had never occurred to her in Cambodia to question the Buddhist doctrines or analyze Buddhist beliefs. She had nothing with which to compare them. Cambodians, in general, practice a blend of Buddhism, animism, and ancestor worship, but think of themselves as Theravada Buddhists. Like many others, Teeda didn't know where Buddhism ended and being Cambodian began.

Buddhist belief, in her mind, was something old people and monks concerned themselves about. She said that perhaps when she grew old she might feel the need to explore it further. Teeda thought of Buddhism as a blend of principles regarding right and wrong behavior; time honored traditions; reverence for ancestors; and belief in reincarnation, the supernatural, animism, and an assortment of other concepts all rolled into one.

She believed some and not the rest. She believed sometimes
and in some settings, but not at other times or in other settings.
To her it was a mixture of beautiful classical dancing, wise
sayings, moral advice, donations of food to the monks, exciting
holidays, wonderful folk tales, and stately buildings with Buddhist
motifs. A person turned to the monks to add dignity to births,
weddings, and funerals. Buddhism was her heritage, almost
indistinguishable from the term Cambodian. What then was
there to challenge or renounce?

30 HALLOWEENS I'VE KNOWN AND LOVED
Roth:

By the time our family arrived in America, my cousin Tevi had
long since forgiven her friends for not telling her what to expect
in her first spook alley. So, when my first Halloween rolled
around several months later, she and Sam (now old hands at all
things American, since they'd been here just over a year) eagerly
explained to Chenda and me what to expect.

My sister and I could hardly wait. We loved candy; imagine,
strangers passed it out free.

A few days before Halloween, Chenda and I bicycled to the
University Mall to gaze at the fantastic costumes in the Pay Less
Drug Store and to buy a few cents worth of candy. We tried on
several masks and a variety of hats. With a magician's hat still
on my head, we turned to the candy across the aisle. After
much debate we made our candy selections, paid for our little
hoard, and were nearly home when a gust of wind blew the
forgotten hat off my head.

Fear gripped us. Would the police think we had stolen the
hat? Why had no one said anything at the check out counter?
You'd think a magician's hat on top of a little boy's head, with
its price tag still dangling, would be obvious to the clerk.
Embarrassed and nervous, we returned to the store, put the hat

on the shelf, and walked out again. Still no one paid us any attention.

A day or two before Halloween we saw our first horror movie. Sitting on the sofa, as tightly packed as sardines in a tin, the family watched *Blackula,* a take-off of the old Dracula movies. Since none of us had any idea who Dracula was, we missed most of the puns, but the scary parts were effective; no one dared take a bathroom break.

By the time my second Halloween came, we'd moved to San Jose. This time, I felt like an old hand at American holidays, too. We plotted how to get the most candy in the shortest amount of time. Later, I learned that American kids also made such plans for maximizing their candy-getting efforts, but ours became a particularly calculated campaign, an outgrowth of the Khmer Rouge years of near-starvation and our constant search for food while under their control.

For me, no costume would do that impeded a fast trot. I decided to be a burglar - regular clothes, my fastest tennis shoes, and just a scarf over my lower face. Chenda insisted on being a princess. I don't remember what our cousins wore. I carried the biggest sack available.

The four of us began our door-to-door assault of the neighborhood as early as our parents allowed and were still going strong until one woman said, "I'm out of candy. Don't you think it is awfully late? It's almost 10 o'clock." Only then did we realize we were the only kids still on the street and sheepishly walked home, but what a pile of candy each of us had.

Swap time. We liked this part almost as much as the acquiring. Sitting in a circle on the living room floor, with our baby sisters and adult relatives looking on, we poured out our loot. My mother couldn't believe the incredible variety or the quantity we'd amassed. Tevi traded for all the Sugar Daddies we would give up. Each of us had favorite candies, and if someone didn't keep a sharp look-out they'd likely find *our* favorites missing from *their* pile.   After pigging out that night, we slept with our remaining treasures near our pillows.

Over the years, like kids all across America, we grew devious enough to think to hide some of our own candy, pretending we'd run out.   After helping the more gullible kids eat theirs, we'd "find" the rest of our candy and eat it too.

Of all the wonderful American holidays, Halloween stands out as my childhood favorite.   I felt cheated I hadn't been part of it years earlier.   Just think how my acquiring skills might have been perfected if I'd started as a preschooler instead of a ten-year-old.

I have regrets over only two Halloweens.   The one when my parents finally convinced me that I was too old to go Halloweening, the end of an era.   And the year I should have been too old but went anyway.

We moved to a new neighborhood that year and I had a new set of friends.   I felt too big to go trick-or-treating with my sisters and cousins, so I joined a group of neighborhood boys.   I wanted to start early again, but one of them said mysteriously, "We have a new tradition here.   There are faster and easier ways to get lots of candy than just going door to door."

We goofed around until quite late, then the boys said, "Time to go."   We went to another neighborhood and waited in the dark till little kids came by with their goodie bags bulging.   Then shouting "trick-or-treat," we swept down on them, grabbed their bags and ran.   Dashing down the streets grabbing bags, we had a wild time.   I was afraid to admit to the others that it really wasn't much fun.   In fact, I thought it was rotten of us to spoil the little kids' Halloween, but the other boys seemed to think it great sport, and I was too much the coward to speak up.

That dimmed the Halloween magic for me, so the next year when my folks suggested that I was too old, I didn't argue much. Instead, I volunteered to take Helena, my youngest sister, so no one could do to her what we had done to those other little kids. I stood half way down the walk while she rang door bells.

Noticing me in the distance (no doubt looking wistful), many who answered the doors said, "Don't you want some candy too?" "Oh, no," I lied, "but thanks anyway."

31 JOBS AND TAXES: MATTERS OF CONFUSION
Teeda:

A well-dressed Cambodian-American moved forward to meet our group of dazed refugees as we stepped from the plane in San Francisco. He wore a suit, ordered us around in Cambodian, and spoke to the Americans in what, in my ignorance, I assumed was faultless English. How, I wondered, did a Cambodian get such an important job in America? His partner impressed me even more. She moved with an assurance and authority I'd never associated with Cambodian women. How did she get those beautiful clothes? Her job must pay lots of money, too, I thought with admiration. Although in Cambodia my father and brothers-in-law had held white-collar jobs, I knew my husband and I didn't have the skills needed to enjoy the same status. There weren't many things Vitou and I knew how to do, so, like most refugees from Cambodia, we assumed we could find work planting and harvesting rice or other crops, much as we'd done under the Khmer Rouge. I didn't know most American farm work was done with the help of machines, not masses of stoop laborers. I envied the couple in the airport and wondered what it took to get such exciting jobs.

Looking back on this scene, I realize how naive I was, totally ignorant of what constituted a high status job in America and oblivious to this couple's broken English and their cheap, ill-fitting, secondhand clothes. They'd probably been in America no more than a year themselves.

It's almost impossible for me to explain to Westerners how ignorant most of us were about how to function in this country or what to expect. It was simply outside my realm of reality, yet I came from a middle-class family who had lived in a city and had more experience with outside cultures and ways of doing things than most Southeast Asians did. The gap you perceive between your experience and ours is not a gap - it's the Grand Canyon!

Most Americans assume that refugees who fled the hell of Southeast Asia, arrive here with *nothing*, by which they mean not much by American standards. But even the poorest American lives better than most people in the world do. Therefore, Westerners seem dumbfounded when I tell them that the *nothing* my husband, my mother, and I brought was one small diamond pendant plus two gold chains, which we hoped to trade for a foothold in America; and we were among the *rich* ones. American friends assumed that anyone with gold or a diamond couldn't be very poor, until I explain that we had nothing else, except the clothes on our backs, and those clothes had been given to us by relief workers at a refugee camp in Thailand.

When the Cambodian man, who met us at the airport, gave each refugee $10 and our onward ticket, we felt wealthy! Imagine a country so rich that people passed out $10 bills to strangers. I wondered what other wonderful things were in store for us.

For the next several years I slipped in and out of a confusing fantasy world when unexpected generosity landed in our laps only to be followed by the harshest of reality. It was hard to make sense of it. For instance, we soon learned that $10 doesn't buy much, and no kind countrymen stepped forward to pass out more. We found fish in abundance in the streams, only to discover it was against the law to take them without paying money for a piece of paper. Even then there were limits on how many could be caught and something called *seasons*. We found fishing too complicated, so we gave up.

We felt pleased when we learned the government had allotted money to refugees for a few years, to help us get established -

these Americans, we thought, what generous people. Like many refugees, we planned to live so frugally that we could save most of the money we received. We wanted to get off government aid as soon as possible. The nest egg we hoped to save would help us start a little business, buy a car, or pay tuition. However, when the welfare department found out, we were penalized for saving. It made no sense to us. Life in America seemed like a roller coaster ride of raised and dashed hopes.

We continually bumped against laws we knew nothing of until we broke them. We found it hard not to be angry with sponsors and others for never explaining such things as taxes, licenses, or unusual laws, or if they did, they should have made sure we understood. These are not things foreigners can deduce. Of course, now I see we must shoulder part of the blame for the communication gap. Americans thought our lack of asking questions meant we understood or agreed. They didn't know how inappropriate Cambodians considered it to question a person of authority or higher status, and in our eyes any Westerner had high status. Such questioning simply isn't done. And Americans routinely mistook our smiling and nodding to mean agreement when it is simply an Asian custom to nod or say "yes," meaning "yes" I heard you, not necessarily "yes" I understand or "yes" I agree.

For the first few years in America, I cleaned homes when I wasn't in school or studying. Shortly before the beginning of our third year in America, one of the women I cleaned for had huge piles of papers cluttering her dining table. When I began straightening them, she quickly told me that those must not be touched. The piles remained for weeks on end and looked unsightly. I finally mentioned this strange practice to a sponsor. She said, "Oh she must be doing her taxes." When I asked what that word meant, Kathryn looked taken aback. "Teeda, haven't you been filing taxes? Don't your employers give you W2 forms?" I didn't know what she was talking about. "I don't have employers," I said, "I just clean people's houses. They give me

$20, and I buy groceries with it on my way home." Just like people did in Cambodia, I traded my services for goods. I could not understand why the government should get involved.

"Well," Kathryn said, regaining her composure, "Vitou now works at Dennis Huntington's service station; he'll send him a W2 statement. When you get it, bring it to me. I'll help you fill out the tax forms."

Vitou and I had noted a difference between the amount Dennis said he would earn and the amount he actually got. In Cambodia we'd have assumed that the boss claimed the money as payment for letting Vitou keep his job, but in America we had an inkling that the money was not pocketed but, instead, somehow went to the government.

Well, Kathryn filled out the tax forms, and, to our total confusion and delight, a few weeks later a check arrived for $99! Elated, I called Kathryn immediately. "Guess what? The government paid us instead of us paying them! I like taxes."

32   MAINTAINING FAMILY CUSTOMS

Joan: Cambodian culture places great importance on the extended family, including those who have died. Let's talk about this from your family's point of view.

Teeda: My mother faithfully maintains an altar in her bedroom. She lovingly created it on the nightstand by her bed. A Buddha statue and a large photo of my father sit on a lace doily. Incense, dry rose petals, and fresh flowers are always there. This shrine holds great meaning for her. It serves as a bridge to our relatives beyond the grave, a place to communicate with my dad who died in a far away land. She cannot visit his grave, but in this way she honors him and is with him.

On special days to remember the dead (similar to America's

Memorial Day), Mum makes a really big deal of it. One time she gave me money to buy a larger altar for my dad, and I forgot. We are so comfortable with her that we don't always pay enough attention, but when we fail in things like that, she gets really upset.

Sometimes when I cleaned house, I didn't put his picture back just right, and once I laid it face down while I worked. She got very upset because she thought I was being disrespectful of my father. And once, when a relative visited us, my mother planned to stay at Mearadey's so the relative could sleep in her room. The relative didn't like the altar; she wanted it moved because it scared her to have it so near the bed. My mother retorted, "It is not scary. It is my husband's altar. You don't have to stay in my room." She felt deeply offended that our relative was scared of my dad's ghost.

Mum prays to my dad to protect the family. Recently, when I had an operation, that altar was alive with incense all the time.

Tevi: When any of us goes somewhere incense is always lit for us. Religion has no real meaning for me, but my grandfather's altar does. I've even begun lighting incense there before exams; I need all the help I can get.

Rasmei: In Cambodia, my father's mother also had an altar. When my cousin had some important event in his life, Grandmother wanted him to come and pray and drink a special water.

Teeda: Among us four sisters, Soorsdey is the most religious. Perhaps religious isn't the right word; she carries on Cambodian traditions best. She doesn't live near us, so she has more need to keep the customs. Also, her husband is involved in the same practices, so they reinforce each other's beliefs. Soorsdey is very much like my mother in placing importance on tradition.

On the other hand, my husband has no belief at all in ghosts, fortune telling, cosmic things. At the Cambodian New

Year each spring, and at other times to remember and honor the dead, I pray for his parents. I think he should remember his parents that way too.

On that day we have a ceremony at home. We cook lots of food and pray to our dead relatives. We cook foods they liked and symbolically serve them at the table as though they were really with us. It is customary to pour water or wine three times - after that it means they are full and we can eat the rest. It is a nice custom.

Rasmei: Not eating before they have eaten is meant to show we respect them and honor them. Even though they have died, we have not forgotten them. It is very important not to be forgotten. If we want some of their favorite food, we ask their permission before taking it.

Tevi: The ceremony itself is like taking time to remember that person.

Teeda: In these ceremonies, we pray to the god to take care of our family. We pray to the spirit to take care of us, and we remember our relatives who have died.

Chenda Poong: When we kids go to these ceremonies we mostly just eat, watch the adults do the ceremonies, and thank our grandfather for everything.

Sam: We take the praying part very seriously; at least I do.

Tevi: When it comes to Grandfather, I take it very seriously too. Because I can't put flowers on his grave or visit it, I honor his memory by lighting incense. It is a reflection of my esteem for him. I think of him at those times; is he successful in what he is doing? is he happy? I'm sure the ceremonies have different meanings for each person, but that is how I feel.

Chenda Poong: Each night before going to sleep, I pray. It is like Grandfather is my personal diary. I tell him what is going on and thank him for keeping us all safe and ask him to continue to help us. I was a two-year-old when I last saw him, but he is very real to me.

Rasmei: Every night I do that too. I have a silent conversation with my father. I pray about things at work or people that upset me; I pray as though he were with me all the time.

Tevi: For me it is not like that. To me what I do at work or school, I do myself. It has nothing to do with Grandfather. I don't carry on conversations with him. But for each person it is different. What they do is right for them.

Teeda: When you talk about religion, Joan, you speak of God. Have you noticed the difference in what we are saying? When we speak of religion in our culture (or at least the Buddhist religion of our family, and I think they might be a bit different) it has always been as a vehicle to get in touch with the person who died.

I was raised to believe, and I still sometimes do believe, that after you die your spirit kind of still hangs around. You are still with the family - kind of. When I saw the movie *Ghost*, it was so real. It touched me in a big way.

Mum, especially, uses Buddhism as a vehicle to talk to her husband. She goes to ceremonies whenever they are available. Why does she do that? It always comes down to "I have to do good things for people so my husband will benefit from what I am doing." She can't do anything for him personally since he isn't here, so Mum and the rest of us try to do many things to pay him back. We owe him a lot and don't ever want him to be ashamed of us.

I don't remember my dad very well, but every time I speak up or assert myself in some way, Mum always says, "You are just like your dad." I feel that I really owe him my being and my personality. He helped me be more assertive. In Cambodia that was considered a negative quality in me, but in America it has helped my career.

Tevi: He is a very strong figure in our family. The thing I remember that was great about him, in terms of the grandfather and grandchild relationship, is that he maintained a distant and dignified manner, but at the same time he joked with us. It wasn't beneath him to play with us grandkids, and he did. He had a great sense of humor. Often a joke was not obvious; it might be just in the look on his face.

Teeda: As Tevi said, my dad still has a very strong influence on our family and so does Mum. My sisters and I love her so much, and so do the grandchildren. I try to figure out her secret. I hope my children will love me like I love her. I think her secret is that she gives all the time. If she has anything she will give it to us. She is fiercely loyal. When the grandkids and their parents have problems she sides with the grandchildren; she backs them all the way. Even when they have done wrong, she doesn't want them to feel excluded.

My dad was the same way. When my sisters married, he didn't want them to live somewhere else. He wanted to keep the family together. So he arranged for them and their husbands to live with us. He paid all the bills. He fed everyone and saw that we had a good life. Our parents just gave and gave, so my family is really attached to them and to each other.

Tevi: Their giving and serving didn't come across as restraining or confining. My grandparents' example has given us values to base our lives on. We like being together. We don't live in the same house as we did in Phnom Penh or as we did at your house in Davis, Joan, but we get together every weekend. Each Sunday we go to a restaurant for brunch.

Teeda: Sometimes we talk about buying land and building a house big enough for all of us or building homes next door to each other.

Tevi: My grandfather was definitely the head of the household, but he didn't act condescendingly to us. It wasn't degrading the way he said things. It is incredible how he did that. All of us wish we knew the secret.

Teeda: Because Mum lives with me, I sometimes lose patience with her ways. Then all the grandchildren jump on me - "Teeda, you can't say that to Grandma." My nieces and nephew blame me for any difficulty that arises. They don't have to put up with her and all the things I have put up with, but they make me stop and think. It is good for me to see the way they defend her.

I realize that what is so special about my mother is that she is so genuine. She is clean and honest. She has a childlike quality and trust about her. She is very smart but naive, and we love and respect her for it. She has our complete loyalty.

Joan: What will happen when Grandmother is gone? She and others of her generation have been the bearers and keepers of the altars and the other family traditions.

Teeda: I'm going to carry on. Right now I don't pay much attention because she's doing it. But I really respect the traditions. Mearadey already has an altar in her house, and when my mother is gone, I'll maintain the one she has at my house. I will add her photo next to my dad's. If Vitou dies before I do, then I'll add his photo to the family altar too.

I don't know what my little children will do when they grow up; Laura and Andrew were born in America and are being raised here. The traditions won't be as much a part of my children's growing up as they were of mine, and certainly not as much as the traditions have been a part of my mother's life. She is more religious now than she ever was in Cambodia. I think it is because my father isn't with us. If he were here, I don't think she would be so zealous.

In Cambodian-American families the decision about my generation maintaining the traditions will depend on how diligently the older generation is maintaining them now. Mum enforces the customs and the altar practice more than anyone I know. For example, many Cambodian-Americans have an altar in the house simply because others do. In contrast, Mum has one because she feels it is where she can communicate with my father.

She has very exacting ideas about what is proper for the altar. One time, for decoration purposes, I tried moving the altar to a table at the foot of the bed where there was more room. She felt deeply offended. She said, "He has to be higher, and he has to be by my head, not my feet." I had to apologize for my ignorance. I'd been cleaning and wanted to give the altar more room and make it prettier. I wanted to please her; instead I'd angered her.

Joan: What will happen in the next generation? That is important for the younger generation of refugees and immigrants, who have been reared in America, to think about and consider carefully. With you, your family's traditions will live or die. For instance, do you grandchildren anticipate carrying on the tradition of maintaining a shrine?

Sam: I think it will be a little hard. It will depend on who we marry. If we marry a Cambodian-American who doesn't believe these things, or if we marry a Caucasian, then it will be hard. Right now I only do it because the adults do it. I don't know if I would do it myself.

Tevi: That is a responsibility each person must take. We'll have to decide to continue it or not. In a way, deciding to carry on the tradition shows respect for the person who has done it before you. It would be a way to show honor for Grandmother and my mother.

33 BOOT CAMP
Narrated by Vitou Mam

Minimal Editing:

I joined the United States Navy Reserve, hoping it would help me get job as aeronautical mechanic. I had graduate from well recognize course and held two licenses - one for the engine, one for rest of the plane. Still, I couldn't find work as mechanic; I lacked on-the-job experience. I heard major airlines like to hire former military mechanic. They like their training, but more important, those mechanic know how to follow orders and work as a team. So, I join the Navy.

When I went to boot camp in San Diego, I knew I would face lots of physical challenge and all that. In Cambodia, I was also in a boot camp when I was a boy soldier. I went when I was thirteen, but that boot camp last only one week. Lots of shooting and running. Then they consider us soldiers. They sent us to fight the Khmer Rouge.

The first shock for me in San Diego: they play games on recruits. They put something on us to trick us. For instance, our uniform have lots of pockets, but we weren't suppose to have anything in them. I know that. They told us. When I put on the new uniform, I check my pockets, but they had trick me. The officer know inspection tag in pocket from factory. Right away they want to intimidate us. From start, they make a point to find things to see your reaction. They try to make you mad, to train your mind. When they find any infraction of the rule, they send us to the heavy duty exercise - extra long workout.

They do all kind of things like that to train the temper of the recruits. They try to train the mind of the young kids. High blood pressure when the kids see they tricked! Soon I understand why they want to trick us, so I not get mad. I had advantage; I was older. Only one recruit older than me.

I hadn't expect they would try to train the mind. In Cambodia I got use to do what you are told. But the navy officer they could still find mistakes. They keep your name in a log book.

They try to get people to lose their temper. Example: in middle of the night they took shaving foam and filled somebody's boot. In the morning the whistle blew. We had five minute till inspection. This guy put his foot in the boot fast. Foam went everywhere. People in charge try to find out who play the practical joke. They couldn't find the person because nobody in our company did it. All day they keep trying to get someone to confess. Nobody confess, so the entire company had to do heavy duty workout. Everybody try to blame each other, try to find out who did it. At the end of boot camp the leader admit they did it just to get our response, to teach recruit to control their temper.

When the leader talk loud right in your face, I would just hold still; most younger guy they got mad and shout back. Extra duty workout for them!

At night if you don't do everything good during the day, you don't get a break. It terrible on you. They do everything to make you get mad fast. Like for example, they tell you, "Fifteen minute for mail." Time to write to family. Then maybe after ten minute they say, "Time up." You almost finish with the writing and you feel annoy. But when they say, "A-ten-hut," you have to get up. If you slow, they take your name. It like prison, no freedom.

My wife so mad at me when I join Navy Reserve. We ran away from one country where they tell you you don't do anything right, and then I volunteer to do that again!

Another surprise - culture shock for me - showers together, all naked. And go to toilet with no walls, no privacy. No privacy in sleeping.

Excellent food for me; those other guy hate the food. They use to their mom's cooking. But I like American food.

I got set back two week because at end of the eight week boot camp I fail English test. Four, five other guy in my company fail too. They make up a new unit from those who fail - about two hundred guy from different companies. We feel like the worst people; we wear a different belt. Other recruits know we didn't pass. We work on English for two week and retake test. You can take the test two time. If you don't pass, you have to go back for two more week. At end of two week I pass test, but now all my shipmate gone ahead. I was assign to company that graduate then. I didn't know these people.

In second company we had a real tough company commander. He want to be number one. He like competition; that's my type. He start to like me.

One week our heavy duty was cooking. You get up at 3 a.m., work hard all day, and get back about 11 p.m. You only get four-five hour sleep.

I got to be a leader. You don't have to do anything, just say "left, right, halt," whatever. I assign people to do this work and that. A lot of them white guy. They get mad for me to tell them. I start to feel discrimination then; I didn't feel discrimination against me when I was one of them. They didn't want to take order from me. I'm not good at giving order either. You can't punish them physically. Key thing I was suppose to do when they didn't do something just right was take their name. I didn't do it. I realize I can't be that kind of leader. If they don't respect me and do what I tell them, probably I end up doing it myself, like when I was manager in the doughnut shop. The girl I told to mop the floor, she didn't want to do it. She did a sloppy job, so I just did it over instead of making her do it right or firing her.

Once you leave boot camp, the military isn't so strict. In reserves we still have to salute all the officer and stuff, but not like boot camp. It is more like civilian job when we do actual work on the plane on my reserve duty weekends. The boss show a lot of power and we have to do what he say quickly. Now I can see why airline like people who have been in military. They like the brain-washing. Skills aren't so important, they can train a mechanic on the spot if needed, but taking order isn't so easy to train.

When I arrive at San Francisco airport after boot camp training, I stop by the United Airline personnel office to upgrade my application. I had file job application with all the airline same time I apply to be a doughnut shop manager, but no one call me. After reserve, I want to try for airline job again. When I stop by the United Airline office, the person there seem impress; I was still in uniform. I had to fill in what kind of plane I work on in the military. Since I hadn't work on them that much, I decide to be vague on the time part. In one week they call me! They send me a package of contract papers, and I got the job.

Some discrimination at work; not much. Now I am a quality control inspector, so if I say job not done right, mechanic must do over. After people read the first book about my family, they are friendlier. When they read the book, they know I was lucky and treat me more like family. One guy want to know more about how I did hunting in jungle. He invite me three time to go hunting, but I don't want to hunt for fun. I had to do it in Cambodia for the Khmer Rouge for a living - to stay alive. Not for fun.

Within six month I move from night shift to swing. Later I could have gone on day shift, but I stay with swing so I could take care of my two children while my wife work days. In 1989, I took test to be an inspector, got train right away and move back to midnight shift. About ten month later I move up to swing shift. Now my children are older, so I move to day shift when that became available. I came to America in 1980; it took nine year, but now I have the job I always wanted.

34 CULTURAL CROSS-TALK

"If you really want it, why not put a bug in your mother's ear?" Teeda's horrified expression let Kathryn know it had happened again - cultural miscommunication. Just imagine the fate of a daughter who dared put a real bug in an honored elder's ear!

We speak idiomatically so routinely that we often fail to notice until someone from another culture focuses our attention; so between chuckles, Kathryn tried again. "You know, drop a hint." Bafflement replaced shock. Teeda thought she understood each word, but could not fathom how to drop something that wasn't an object. "Put the idea in her head" met with raised eyebrows. One more try: "Why don't you suggest, mention in a subtle way, that you've been wanting such a gift?" Suddenly, this newcomer's eyes lit up; words and meaning meshed.

The first few times that Teeda's niece Tevi said, "Take a short walk on a long pier," I assumed her tongue had simply raced ahead of her thoughts. When she continued to use the phrase incorrectly, I decided I'd better explain that the idiom "take a long walk on a short pier" meant jump in the lake, get lost, you're all wet, scram. Fortunately, she'd been in America long enough by then to understand the other expressions I'd used to explain the first.

Not surprisingly, recent arrivals have trouble with many words, especially our idioms and slang, just as we do with theirs. However, even a person who has lived in this country many years and speaks English fluently may still have gaps in their knowledge. They find themselves confronting new words or hearing everyday words imperfectly and derive the wrong meaning.

For instance, my biochemist husband sent his Cambodian-American research assistant, Nat, to the supermarket to buy a head of cauliflower for the next experiment in the laboratory. At the time, Nat was a bright college senior pulling down top grades and had been in the country more than a decade. Before leaving for the store, Nat asked, "Does it matter what color I buy?" Taken aback, my husband replied, "Well, don't get yellow, that's old. It should be as white as possible." To the delight of his lab mates, instead of buying cauliflower, Nat returned with a bunch of daisies - white colored flowers.

When I told Teeda's sister Rasmei about Nat's misunderstanding, she said that she had made a similar mistake in a class for newcomers. One morning the teacher asked "What did you eat for breakfast today?" The students practiced their oral skills by responding in turn. Struggling over each word Rasmei replied innocently, "I . . . ate . . . the . . . kitchen," when she meant to say "chicken." Apparently, this is a common mistake;

half the class heard nothing wrong, the other half burst into laughter. The teacher merely nodded.

Teeda then told about the first time her English class took turns presenting conversations between two people. She and the handsome young Vietnamese fellow who sat behind her stood when it was their turn. Thinking only of something to say in English, not the social implications, Teeda began the conversation by asking, "Hi. what's your phone number?" Trying to ignore the ripple of laughter in the room, he replied, "Home phone?" "Ya." Her classmates teased, "Teeda, won't your husband be jealous?"

But misunderstood words is not restricted to crossing languages. Even people from English-speaking nations often talk past each other. For instance, I had to listen hard as a London "cabby" excitedly described a truck and automobile accident in which the lorry's bonnet hit the boot of the Mini Morris, causing the motorcar to leave the tarmac, cross the verge, and end up in a hedge with its petrol leaking. And *that* would cost more than a bob to fix.

When we lived in Australia, a teenaged daughter almost slapped a fellow's face before she realized he wasn't being vulgar when he repeatedly interrupted her narration with "Fair-dinkum!" - the Aussie version of "Right on!" or "Really?"

An English woman visited me several years ago, and after dinner asked, "May I spend a penny?" "What?" I asked. Looking a little desperate she repeated, "May I spend a *penny*?" Words and meaning came together for me just in time; remembering that public toilets in England used to require a big copper penny in the slot, I directed her to my bathroom.

We must learn to mentally edit what we say if we hope to communicate with people from other backgrounds, even other native born Americans. In a nation as large and diverse as the United States, it should surprise no one that wonderfully colorful regional speech patterns develop. My seat companion on a long bus ride hailed from western Pennsylvania. She used the phrase, "red the room" several times and acted surprised when I finally asked for an explanation. She was talking about housecleaning, getting the room "ready" for guests.

If English speakers find deciphering each other's meaning difficult, people whose native language is not English must find it nearly impossible at times. Setting aside American idioms, jargon, and unusual phrases, imagine how difficult it is for foreigners simply to master the meaning of our ordinary words when so many are spelled the same or sound alike yet have unrelated meanings. For example, Rose is a girl's name, a flower, a color, or something the stock market did. Then there are the words that sound like rose. We plant vegetables in rows, but that word also refers to an action John does in a boat. Roes are small European deer, while Roe's means something belonging to Mr. Roe. But roe are fish eggs.

Dice becomes die when you have one, but die is also death, while dye refers to a color or a process, and in England, Di is a Princess. Birds flew, you are sick with the flu, but smoke goes up the flue. A teacher calls the roll, eats a cinnamon roll, gives the ball a roll, or auditions for the leading role. And I hope never to be asked to explain about the fellow who showed mettle when he dared meddle with the general's metal medal.

Translating too literally between languages also gives rise to confusion. For instance, my son once feasted on a delicious, filling meal prepared by his French hosts. When pressed for more, he shook his head, patted his stomach, and foolishly made a direct translation, "No thanks, I'm full." Seeing his hosts' shocked looks, he realized he'd used the wrong form of *full.* Instead of saying, "I ate well," he'd said, "I'm pregnant." Quite a startling pronouncement from a young man.

Asians often consider Westerners blunt and direct. We come right to the point with few preliminaries, a most un-Asian thing to do. At work, Teeda must critique others' performance as part of the annual staff reviews. She finds it difficult to be straightforward in her reports, especially if they are negative. Her gentle, less than forthright report on a middle-aged, white, male co-worker finally drove her boss to ask a colleague to speak to her about the problem. He did so by saying, "Teeda, you've got to stop beating around the bush. You must learn to call a spade a spade." Understanding only the general drift of these phrases, Teeda said a little too loudly, "Okay, I agree; he's a spade." The noisy office fell silent, then her colleagues burst into laughter.

Co-workers again enjoyed Teeda's original use of idioms when she told them that she hated it when people stabbed you behind your back.

If you've ever struggled to communicate in a language other than your native tongue, you'll readily appreciate others' efforts to talk Americanese, even if they put the em-PHAS-is on the wrong syl-LAB-le or otherwise slaughter the language. Give them *half a chance* and you'll both be richly rewarded. New-found friends and shared laughter over misunderstood words should be compensation enough but, occasionally, you also might receive a tangible reward, such as I did when my husband presented me with a beautiful bouquet of white daisies, and it wasn't even my birthday. Thanks Nat!

35 TV's TWICE-TOLD CITIZENSHIP CEREMONY

Sandra Gin Yep reported from San Jose for Sacramento KCRA Channel 3's evening news, July 24, 1986. The camera panned the audience then zoomed in on the person at the lectern when the ceremony began.

A Court Official: Would everybody please take out their "Green Cards,"* you will be turning them in today.

Vitou, speaking to Sandra Gin Yep: I'm proud to be an American - especially this country, you know, the best in the worl'.

Teeda: This place is a great place to make your own life, to be the best.

Sandra: It's been a long journey for Teeda and Vitou Mam to return their "Green Cards." We last met them when they and their family arrived at Sacramento's Metropolitan Airport in 1980, penniless, jobless, but just the same thrilled to be here. . . . Eleven years ago they and millions of Cambodians were run out of the capital city of Phnom Penh by communist troops . . . forced into four years of slavery at labor camps known as the killing fields. . . . Despite starvation, disease, and wholesale executions the family endured, pretending to be lowly peasants, part of the faceless masses toiling in the rice paddies. Was your life threatened?

Teeda: Ya. Ya, all the time 'cause people that work with you was being taken away and killed every day, like my father.

Sandra: Two daring escape attempts ultimately carried them out of the holocaust to a refugee camp in Thailand and then to America. Today they hold down successful jobs in the Bay Area.

---

* "Green Cards" are issued to newcomers to whom the United States government has granted Permanent Resident status. If a person is later granted citizenship, the green card is returned to the government.

A Court Official: . . . and that you take this obligation freely
without any mental reservation or purpose of evasion: So
help you God.

Immigrants in unison: I do.

Sandra: Joan Criddle of Davis . . . says their harrowing story
inspired her to write a book. . . .

Joan: [What I find remarkable is their] ability to survive
incredible obstacles and fear without animosity and hatred;
to come out of that with not so many scars - to be beautiful
human beings.

Sandra: Teeda and Vitou are also looking forward to another
important event in their lives - the arrival of their first born,
the next generation to enjoy the freedom and opportunities
that they've come to cherish in this country.   At the U.S.
Federal Building in San Jose, Sandra Gin Yep for Channel
3 reports.

Roberto Munoz of San Jose's KNTV News 11 filed a similar
report that same evening.

Doug Moore, Anchorman: One hundred and six men, women
and children became American citizens today during
swearing in ceremonies held at the Federal Court House in
downtown San Jose.   Among them a couple whose story of
survival and escape to freedom is the subject of a soon to
be released book.   News 11's Roberto Munoz has the story.

Roberto: Vitou Mam and his wife, Teeda, were a little nervous
this morning.   And who could blame them.   After all, they
were about to take the big step of becoming American
citizens.   For Vitou and Teeda, today's swearing in
ceremony is the fulfillment of an impossible dream, a dream
that began as a nightmare.

Teeda: I reach a point where I knew it jus' a matter of time that
I die.

Roberto: Teeda and Vitou still have painful memories of when
their native Cambodia was overrun by the Communist

Khmer Rouge. To this day, no one really knows how many people were slaughtered between 1975 and '79; all Vitou remembers is his neighbors being taken away during the night.

Vitou: They never return, and they [the Khmer Rouge] never tell people that these people gonna get kill.

Roberto: Realizing that they too would be killed, Vitou and Teeda escaped by walking more than three hundred miles to the Thai border.

Teeda: Also, sometime we just walk 'cross battle between the Vietnamese and the Khmer Rouge. But I think our will was so strong to get out of our country because we knew that if we live there longer, our life is not guarantee. . . .

Roberto: [T]he refugee couple . . . came to this country six years ago. Since then, they have learned English, he as gotten a job with United Airlines, and she now works as a computer software analyst with Symantec of Cupertino.

Joan: I'm so proud. Because Vitou doesn't have family, I feel like his mother, and this *was* a special day.

A Court Official: . . . that you will support and defend the Constitution and the laws of the United States against all enemies, foreign and domestic.

Unanimous: I do.

Permissions granted by Jan Young, KCRA
& Roberto Munoz, KNTV

36 GRANDMOTHER

Tevi:

Grandmother is cagey; she finds ways to get the attention she wants. Endlessly it seems, she tricks us into helping her run errands, usually by not telling us all her plans in advance. We keep falling into her trap, even when we suspect she is laying one. But then, how could we refuse to help her with "just one little project," and then just one more, when no single project takes more than a few minutes? How can we say we don't have time to drive her to pick up "just this one little thing?" yet suspecting that *one thing* will expand to ten before we're done.

One time she asked me to drive her to the dressmaker's - Grandma wears only Cambodian dresses. Hoping to get out of taking her I countered, "Grandma, I don't know how to get there, besides I don't have much time." "Come on Monkey, it will take only a minute. You just drive. I know the way." I was leary, but she acted so sure of the directions that I let myself believe her. I'd gone there with my mom a couple of times, so I got us to the general area and drove around but couldn't find the house.

I said, "Okay Grandma, I'm lost. Where is it?" "I don't know." "What do you *mean* you don't know? You insisted you knew exactly where she lived." She shrugged. "Just give me the house number then," I said. "I don't know it." "Grandma, how am I supposed to find the place if you don't know where it is and don't have a house number?"

She finally remembered she had the phone number in her purse, so I asked a stranger if I could use her phone. Grandmother doesn't speak English, so she sat serenely in the car while I did the embarrassing leg work. Not recognizing the street name that the seamstress gave me, I hoped she'd given good directions. She hadn't. When we arrived in what was supposed to be the right neighborhood, the street name was different. I drove around and around the blocks until I saw I house I thought I recognized.

Grandmother said, "I don't remember the rose bushes being so small." With an edge in my voice I said, "I *think*, Grandma, this is the house." I didn't remember the wrought iron fence but decided it was probably installed recently. We rang the doorbell. Nobody answered. Since I'd just talked to the woman, and she expected us, I finally admitted we'd come to the wrong place. Still Grandma refused to give up. I drove around some more. Finally, I asked a man mowing his lawn if he recognized that street name. He did; it was a couple of blocks further along the same street, where the road jogged and the name changed.

The next time Grandmother conned me into a wild goose chase, she wanted a favorite Cambodian pastry that a friend of hers makes. "I don't know Grandma. Are you *sure* you know how to get there?" I teased her about our dressmaker trip, but she insisted that this time she really knew where the woman lived. Since I knew it wasn't far away, I decided she probably did. We got in the car, and I said, "Okay, which way do I go?" She pointed left. At the next intersection I said, "Which way now?" She pointed right. Before long we were on the main road that passes our subdivision, and I asked again. She replied, "I'm not sure. I know it is past the school." When we got there, she perked up again and said, "Turn here, it looks about right . . . ; no, turn back, this doesn't look familiar. . . ." We drove back and forth as she tried to zero in on the house. Finally I said, "I'm going to take us home. Just call her. *When* you have directions, I'll take you."

I used to tend my Aunt Teeda's children during the summer, but I spent more time running errands for Grandma than I did taking care of Laura and Andrew - Grandma lives with Teeda's family. One day Grandmother said she'd watch the kids while I went to the grocery store for her. Once I'd agreed to that, she told me to pick up her medicine at the pharmacy as well. Then came the real request. She wanted a special Asian perfume.

"Now wait a minute, Grandma," I protested. "Why do you want perfume? You never use it." "I want to put it in some powder to make the powder smell good." "Grandma, you're going to send me all over hunting for some perfume called *Champagne* that probably isn't even sold in America." She merely beamed her innocent smile at me. I must have gone to every Asian store in Silicon Valley before I found it.

Grandmother can be exasperatingly headstrong, manipulative, and domineering. She could drive us crazy with her constant maneuverings and devious ways if we focused on them. Instead, we've chosen to find them endearing and to joke about them. Grandma will always be a little Cambodian woman who just happens to live in America. She'll never change and we know it. We allow her the luxury of enveloping herself in Cambodian custom from head to toe, not something easily accomplished in this country. To humor her, we chase all over town getting the food she's hungry for, the incense she insists on for the little shrine by her bed, or the *Champagne* perfume she considers "just right." She is truly the matriarch of our extended family. We all know it and gladly give her that respect.

Despite the inconvenience, I've learned to enjoy her blatant manipulation and tease her about it. Sometimes it is so naively apparent what she is trying to do, that I can't help but go along with it and neither can anyone else. She almost always gets her way, and people don't even really mind giving it to her. In the family we marvel at her ability and wish we had the same gift.

She has always been a warm, loving person with a need to interact, to be seen for herself and not be just one of the crowd. Even in America with her limited language ability, she finds ways to control the situation and to build meaningful relationships with those she meets. For years, she and our sponsors have communicated almost entirely through hugs, pats, smiles, and tears. Anyone who knows Grandmother Ean Bun soon learns that love knows no language barrier.

She is very intelligent but never outgrew a charmingly innocent, genuine, childlike quality. It draws people and makes them want to cater to her. Seemingly without effort, she trains everyone to accommodate to her ways. Even strangers. Stores reduce their prices for her. Her dentist has learned to say, "Open" in Cambodian so she will understand. His receptionist now knows to book Grandma for an extra long time slot; she won't be rushed and likes to visit. Her physician fills out insurance forms for her and personally sees that his receptionist makes her next appointment. Grandma just sits smiling sweetly, accepting the help as her due.

Recently, I've been the one to take Grandma to the doctor - she's one of the world's great hypochondriacs. She especially likes her new physician, Doctor Smith, whom she calls "Doctor Smit." Several months passed between her first and second visit yet she assumed this busy man would remember her. I said, "Grandma, he has lots of patients. He won't remember you." She kept insisting, "He know me. Dr. Smit, he know me." She was right, of course.

When we got to the building, she asked, "Where Dr. Smit room?" "I don't know, Grandma. You'll have to show me. Mom brought you last time, remember; I've not been here before." So we walked up and down the halls in this large clinic until she stopped in front of a door and asked, "Does that say Smit?" It did.

Although no other patients were in the waiting room, we sat there more than an hour. We could not understand the delay until Dr. Smith opened the door and motioned to Grandma. He explained that he'd been trying desperately, but without success, to locate a translator. He hadn't realized that's why I'd come.

Smiling broadly and pointing proudly to me, she took him by the sleeve and said, "Grrr-aand-children, grrr-aand-children." In the examining room they joked awhile, with me as go-between. Then, while she patted him in her typical, motherly way, he gave her a series of injections for her arthritis. As the shots continued, Grandma (without noticing what she was doing) gave him one of her notorious squeezes - fingernails digging deeper and deeper into the flesh of his arm - as she tried to control the pain. Her dentist is another recipient of this same increasingly painful gouge whenever he repairs her teeth.

Wanting an excuse to continue the visit with Dr. Smith when the injections ended, she kept up a stream of Cambodian while she pantomimed that she had a bad back. As part of their ongoing banter, he told her he had backaches too. When he turned away to write a prescription, she began massaging his back, saying in her broken English, "Me very good massage. Me very good massage." She really does give excellent massages that everyone in the family appreciates and so did Dr. Smith, I hope.

He told me to bring her back in four months. I don't know how she knew what he said to me, but she looked at him, raised two fingers, and with a wicked twinkle in her eye said, "Two." "No," he countered, accepting her challenge, "Four, four" "Two, two," she kept insisting. "Three," he finally countered, waving three fingers at her. She triumphantly accepted his compromise. No wonder she is so sure he remembers her.

Recently on a visit, Dr. Smith told her to stop taking the pills for high blood pressure, and to cut back on salt. A few days later, she called me to ask if she could take the pills. I explained again what the doctor said, but she complained of symptoms and felt sure they'd cure the problem. "No, Grandma. You must not take those pills." Then she tricked me into taking her to the doctor by saying she had some other pills that should work, but she wanted "Dr. Smit" to look at them to be sure. I decided to humor her, thinking it would take less time. However, at the office our half hour became almost three. She'd conned him into giving her a complete physical. It's good she can't speak English; no telling what she'd get away with then.

When we left Dr. Smith's office after that marathon visit, she dragged me to the pharmacy to get the new medicine. Then she insisted we stop for mangos for my other grandma, my father's mother, who'd just arrived from Cambodia. Once in the grocery store, she said, "Oh, let me get . . . " I thought I'd never pry her out of the store. She likes to shop and especially likes American supermarkets. Then she wanted to buy a wok. I put my foot down on that plan. "No Grandma. I'm going to let Teeda help make that decision. I really have to get home."

Grandma loves spending money. A habit of hers in prewar Cambodia, too, my mother and aunts tell me. She particularly enjoys buying gifts for others. When Vitou visited Hong Kong, Grandma had him buy presents for her doctor and dentist. She considers them personal friends. Each also receives a Christmas gift from this elderly patient, one I'm sure they'll never forget.

Her only income is a small Social Security check, but it goes a long way because her daughters and sons-in-law meet all her expenses. My sisters, cousins, and I learned early that if our parents denied us something we wanted to buy, Grandma would slip us the money.

Grandmother spends love just as lavishly. But we've discovered there is a price to be paid for this unconditional love of hers; she's tied our hearts to her so tightly we would do anything for her. So when Grandma requests a "little favor," we now understand we are really being asked to spend an entire afternoon - or longer.

37 THE FAMILY DISCUSSES RELIGION

<u>Joan:</u> Coming from a Buddhist background, your family's religious concepts are quite different from many Westerners', and each of you approaches religion in your own way. Let's talk about that.

<u>*Tevi:*</u> My first experience with religion was as a little girl in Phnom Penh. My great-grandmother Butt, my grandfather's mother, lived with us. She recited Buddhist scripture in Sanskrit to me, and liked me to memorize the words and recite them to her. I didn't know the language, but when she recited a passage once, I could easily repeat it. I became her favorite pupil because I learned so fast, but it meant nothing to me. I don't think my great-grandmother even understood much of what she recited; nonetheless, I could tell that reciting it meant a lot to her. I enjoyed our time together, especially that she was pleased with me.

None of us kids had a religious background. It was not part of our upbringing, especially not after the Khmer Rouge came to power. We had almost no contact with religion in Cambodia, so, of course, when we came to America we didn't understand the significance of what we did at church or even that it was supposed to have significance. Therefore, activities associated with religion here have had little meaning for us.

<u>*Mearadey:*</u> Nobody explained Buddhist beliefs or that there were differences among Buddhists in different parts of the world. Even though my mother occasionally talked about being a Buddhist, I don't think she really had a clear understanding either.

<u>*Rasmei:*</u> We just went to the temple and followed what the monks did. We listened and repeated Sanskrit, but we understood only a few simple words of that language.

<u>Joan:</u> Mearadey, didn't you and Ken have some idea about what you were agreeing to when you made the decision for your family to become Lutherans? You understood it was a

religion, didn't you?

Mearadey: We knew our family had been sponsored to America by a religious group. Later, when the pastor and others met with us, we kind of knew they were trying to teach us about their beliefs, but we understood only some of what they talked about. Other people's religious concepts are difficult to understand even with no language or cultural barrier.

Tevi: Besides, all our thoughts and efforts focused on our immediate needs of trying to adjust to all the strange things in this country. And we were worried about our relatives still in danger in Southeast Asia. That is what mattered to us then.

Mearadey: When we joined the Lutheran Church, Ken and I understood that the baptism ceremony had a religious dimension. To us, however, joining was a way to thank our sponsors for their help. It was a way to fit in. Other refugees had already told us that joining a sponsor's church made them happy. It could help us to learn English and be part of the American community. Church was a place to interact with our new friends. That was very important to us. Regular attendance was a good opportunity to become socialized into American customs, a place for our daughters to engage in worthwhile, wholesome activities, meet nice friends, and learn good things.

I was vaguely aware that a discrepancy existed between our sponsors' understanding of what our baptism meant and our own understanding of its benefits to us. But we were too busy adjusting to America to explore the different expectations further. They didn't seem important.

Joan: What was the response of you girls to becoming Christians?

Tevi: To tell the truth, I didn't know what being a Christian meant. I didn't even know I was going to Christian services for a long time. Everything they did was alien to me. As an eleven-year-old, I had no idea there was a point to the meetings. We sang and heard stories, but to me it was just one more American activity. I went through the motions, doing what our friends did. I liked the social activities best. I didn't mind the lessons, but they weren't as much fun.

Church services were okay, but I wondered why they were held on Sundays of all days, the one day I could relax and take it easy. Sunday was just a weekly holiday from school as far as I was concerned. In Davis, I missed a few Sunday School classes because I wanted to sleep in. I'd have gone more often if the services had been on another day and not so early. Sam, though, was a really good student; she got a Bible because she went often enough to earn one. I didn't.

Mearadey: Church members came to the house and tried to explain their religion to all of us, I guess, but we didn't really catch on. The words and concepts were too difficult for us to understand.

Tevi: We had come to a strange country. We were trying to deal with culture shock, learn a new language, and understand the customs. It never occurred to us to ask about the history of religion. Our needs were much more immediate. It is strange now to look back and realize that neither we nor the church members understood that they spoke past us so completely. We did not even begin to comprehend what they were talking about, but we didn't know it then. We didn't have knowledge of any group's religious history or beliefs, certainly not differences among the various kinds of Christians.

In going to church and being baptized, it didn't occur to me that we were now considered Christians, and by implication that we understood and believed all the things they talked about. Baptism - putting water on my head - why do they want to do that, I wondered. But I didn't openly question their custom. It was just another thing I went along with.

Joan: In America do you have a religious dimension to your life? Are you Buddhists here?

Unanimous: No.

Teeda: We don't think of ourselves as Buddhists, but we still carry on and enjoy many of the customs; it is more of a cultural thing. You probably think of what we do as part of being Buddhist, but we think of it more as following Cambodian traditions.

Roth: What taught me a lot about religion was watching the movie *The Ten Commandments.* After seeing that, I said, "Oh, now I know what religion is all about." I'd heard that part of the Old Testament in Sunday School.

Tevi: For me religion is just history, and everyone has their own version of God. It is a personal thing, even if you don't define just what "god," or nature, or whatever is. My freshman year in college I wanted to learn more about my cultural roots, so I took a course in Eastern religions. To me it was a history course. I found it interesting, but not something that had greater meaning.

I learned a lot in college. Up until then, I had tried to fit in and be just like other Americans. But in college I wanted to know more about my own culture and be my own person. I think religion is different for each person; it is like a relationship. It means different things to different people. As you listen to our family, you can tell that some of us attach quite a bit of meaning to spiritual things and others of us do not. I guess it is like any other family. I realize religion is a very sensitive issue. The thing I have problems with is when people try to convert me. They don't seem to realize that I consider religious belief personal; you have to leave another person's beliefs alone.

Roth: I don't mean to offend anyone, but religion just doesn't have any meaning to me.

Chenda Poong: I believe there is a God, and I believe that my grandfather [who is dead] is real. In America, when I was in seventh grade, I really thought a lot about death and dying. I couldn't stop, even though I tried. I had nightmares about death. I kept thinking about what would happen to me if my parents died or I died. I got really worried; it was hard to concentrate on anything else. It was ruining my life. So one day I went over to my grandmother's to her altar. My grandfather's picture and a Buddha statue are part of the shrine in her bedroom. I prayed, "God, help me. I don't want to think about death any more." That night when I went to sleep, the dreams stopped completely. Every time people talk about religion, I think about that experience, and it makes me believe. I think my grandfather, God, and Buddha helped me.

Rasmei: When we were trying to escape from Cambodia the second time, it was really bad. We almost didn't make it. I prayed to the Buddha to please help us. I promised the Buddha that I would shave my head if we made it to safety in Thailand. Hair was very important to Cambodian women; we were proud of our beautiful long hair. Offering to shave your head was commonly done as a way of offering thanks for special blessings or to do penance. It is a very serious sacrifice. As soon as we got to Thailand, I shaved my head. I believe that my father and the Buddha really helped us escape, otherwise we could not have made it. Remember? My hair was still short five months later when we got to California.

Teeda: One of the most sensitive things we had to deal with when we came to America was having two groups of sponsors, the Lutheran Church group that sponsored Mearadey's family, and the five Mormon families who sponsored the rest of us. We were so relieved when you guys weren't upset with us for being baptized as Lutherans. Since Ken and Mearadey's family were already Lutherans, we decided we should be too. We wanted to be together. Instead of trying to figure out what we actually believed and then making our own decisions, we were somehow trying to pay back favors. We didn't know any better.

In Cambodia, we were treated so badly. The Khmer Rouge squeezed everything out of the population and lied to us constantly. We had a hard time trusting people when we came to America. At first we could not understand our sponsors' motives, but we were grateful for all the help. So any time we could do favors, we wanted to do them. We wanted to make everyone happy.

Rasmei: I had no idea at all what was going on when we got baptized. We just did it because Mearadey's family had. I still have my baptism certificate.

Teeda: In our culture when you call yourself Buddhist, you don't commit to anything. You just say you are a Buddhist. There is no ceremony; there is nothing like baptism to become a member. At least, I don't know of any.

Rasmei: Cambodians are taught to honor their ancestors and the older living members of the family. We were Buddhist because our grandparents were. Older people in Cambodia tended to think about religion more. They got very upset if the younger generations did something they considered wrong - like my grandmother Butt. Every eighth day, I think, she fasted like the Buddhist monks; she ate only in the morning. Then she didn't eat again until the next morning.

Unfortunately, I often did things that made my grandmother angry without knowing beforehand that it would or really understanding why. She always said, "Why do you do that? You are a Buddhist; you should pray to Buddha." That is all I know about Buddhism. I knew I was a Buddhist because she said I was.

Teeda: Joining the Lutheran Church had to do with what we understood to be Ken and Mearadey's sponsors' expectations. We didn't know what was expected of us in America, so when we came to a new country and people suggested we do something, we just did it. We didn't think it through. It is not the Cambodian custom to question or challenge our elders or those in authority. That is considered rude. Under the Khmer Rouge we certainly didn't openly question or challenge anything they told us; it could cost our lives.

In Cambodia friendship and other relationships are based on the exchange of favors. We want to do nice things for people who have been thoughtful or helpful to us; it is a way to honor them. It is a way to win favor with those in authority. In America, we always tried to go to church. We thought it was like a duty or something. It showed respect to our sponsors.

Before we got baptized, the pastor came to our house like he had done for Mearadey's family. He read us stories from the Bible, mostly from the New Testament. To us they were just stories; we never got the concept that they were meant to give us a belief in Christ. We wondered why he read us these stories. Once he told about someone being blind and magical things happened to him and he could see. We sat and listened to all those Bible stories, but we never related to them or realized that he considered the stories true.

In our culture, we also have many myths and legends that explain how the world started and what happens to good people and bad people. Animals and many-armed, multi-headed creatures do fantastic things. There are lots of ghosts, gods, demons, magic, and other things in those stories. Bible stories seemed similar.

When we were baptized, we totally missed the point. For us it was a ceremony, but not a commitment. It was much later before we understood what had been expected of us. Then we felt bad. It is not that we weren't honest; we just didn't know. I feel bad because we kind of defeated the pastor's purposes and what he was trying to have happen.

Roth: Because we sometimes went to social activities at your church, I thought we belonged to it as much as to the Lutheran Church. In my mind, I'd not separated the social activities from the religious instruction and ceremonies. So when people said, "What church do you go to?" I told them both. No wonder they looked at me funny.

Teeda: Without meaning to, the sponsors put us in an awkward position, but at the time, neither we nor they fully understood how awkward it was. It was just a cultural misunderstanding.

Roth: I learned about another strange religious custom just a year or so ago. That's when I went to live with the Gardners in Utah for a semester when I was in high school. I didn't know Mormons fasted once a month. The first Sunday I stayed with them was Fast Sunday. I'd gone to the kitchen early and made myself a huge scrambled egg breakfast and sat down to eat just as Kathryn came in. I asked if she wanted to join me for breakfast. "Oh," she said, "I guess I forgot to tell you that we are fasting. We skip two meals." Mormons don't eat from Saturday night until Sunday night. They donate the money those meals would cost to help the poor.

From then on I fasted with them each month. They didn't ask me to, but I didn't want to be different. I could show respect for them that way. But I didn't tell them that each Saturday night, after everyone went to bed, I sneaked downstairs to make myself a couple of huge sandwiches. I ate them in my room before I went to sleep.

38   TRAVEL ABROAD

Rasmei:

I grew up in Cambodia knowing we were the best, the most advanced country in the region, if not in the world. Our leaders repeatedly told us so. It took a mere two hour flight from Phnom Penh to Hong Kong and just nine days there to dispel that myth for me. A deep sense of betrayal replaced my pride in Cambodia, and I began distrusting the government from then on.

Leng and I had gone to Hong Kong for a delayed honeymoon in 1969, about two months after we married. It took that long just to get passports and other documents cleared through our inefficient government offices. Because Leng worked at the airport, he could travel abroad inexpensively but, until our marriage, had never done so. He had worked for the international airport for thirteen years, yet had never even taken a vacation. He is a workaholic and not fond of travel, so Hong Kong was the first taste of the world beyond our borders for both of us. I was sixteen and Leng twenty-six.

I couldn't sleep the first night, couldn't even stay in the hotel because I found the city so exciting. I enjoyed looking at everything. "Two hours, just two hours," I kept saying in amazement and frustration, throughout the trip. "Just two hours away and yet Cambodians don't know such things exist."

Yes, we had cars, buses, a few nice department stores, and big office buildings in Phnom Penh and in a couple of other cities, but that was about where the similarities ended. All else in Hong Kong seemed bigger, better, or something we'd never even heard of before. Every new thing fascinated me, especially escalators. Imagine, stairs that moved.

My disenchantment with our government intensified when I saw the wonders of Europe the next year. Our leaders had compared Phnom Penh with Paris and said it was better, even better than cities in America. Except for a few wealthy Cambodians who'd traveled abroad and knew otherwise, the rest of us had been gullible enough to believe these statements.

A year after our honeymoon in Hong Kong, Leng took a three month training course in Europe. Since his air fare and living expenses were covered by the Cambodian government, it cost little more for me to join him. I jumped at this once-in-a-lifetime opportunity to go to Europe. Except for my father, who had once been to China as part of an official Cambodian delegation, Leng and I were the only ones in our family to have traveled abroad.

My going to Europe meant leaving our three-month-old baby with Leng's mother and sister. Perhaps I was too young to be a responsible mother, but I didn't even feel guilty leaving our son.

He would be in more experienced hands than mine, I reasoned. I'd married a cousin, so knew my mother-in-law well.

Leng and I lived in inexpensive hotels on their upper, cheaper floors to stretch his living allowance as far as possible. We stayed longest in Lyons were he attended courses in airport administration. We also lived in Paris and London a short time in connection with his work.

Leng went to class until mid-afternoon. To pass the time until he returned, I occasionally went shopping but felt too insecure to venture far from our hotel. I spoke French, but not well. As a very shy seventeen-year-old in a foreign country, I usually stayed in the room reading magazines and books or writing letters. I sent dozens of letters to friends and relatives and wrote my father daily.

Although I loved our trip and all the interesting things I saw and did, I suffered from homesickness. I missed my family and my baby who would be six months old by the time we returned. Leng took me somewhere in the afternoons or evenings so I'd have something to look forward to each day. He knew quite a few people in France's Cambodian community, and we visited tourist attractions.

Our three months in Europe gave us time to judge for ourselves that Cambodia was no match for France or England. In truth, ours was probably one of the more backward nations in the world. That came as a real shock.

When we returned to Phnom Penh, I told my parents, cousins, sisters, friends, and anyone else who would listen that we'd all been fed a big lie. I told them, "Look at our country; it might have lots of trees and beautiful scenery, but our government stinks. What is it doing to help the average person? Leaders pass out a few trinkets when they tour the villages, but where are the factories? Where is the industry? Where are the public schools and transportation? Where are the doctors and the medical clinics in the countryside? The government should help start something to make life better for more Cambodians." Our country had great potential, but the leaders ignored the needs of the people in the villages, fed them lies, and kept them ignorant. They spent too much money on grandiose boulevards to make Phnom Penh a showplace. It made me so angry. Conditions had to be bad when even a young adult could see the problems our government should address and did not.

I hated the custom of using money and influence to buy power. I wanted things to be fair. Getting a good job should be based on skill, education, or training, not on bribes and favors. Yet unqualified men made decisions for the country based on what would line their own pockets, not on what benefitted the nation. The Cambodia in which I was reared was filled with graft and corruption. Many people in the cities grew discontent with this regime, but not the rest of the population. They were lulled with the leaders' lies.

Government officials continued to make speeches on the radio telling Cambodians we were better than other countries. Bragging, always bragging. My two trips abroad had opened my eyes to advances in other nations and to compare those advances with problems Cambodia faced. Unfortunately, the 1970 coup did not change the situation much. Graft and corruption continued; inefficiency had become a way of life. Escalating civil war, inflation, and the spill-over fighting from the war in Vietnam made the situation even worse. Many outlying areas came under the communist Khmer Rouge control after 1970, and by late 1974, when I was a twenty-two-year-old mother of two, the government controlled only the cities. Then on April 17, 1975, the Khmer Rouge rebels took Phnom Penh, the capital city. The war ended, the cities were forcibly emptied, and a four-year-long night of horror descended.

As a slave under the Khmer Rouge, I continued to travel - but only in my mind. The stoop labor I did each day exhausted me physically but required nothing of me mentally. We weren't supposed to talk to those who worked with us; it used energy that should be put to productive labor. I had to have something to occupy my mind, so I blocked out our detestable existence by concentrating on good times in my life and relishing details of the trips I'd taken.

While I planted and harvested rice, I, silently recited French words, hour on end. I didn't want to forget how to read and write the language - if only I could spend as much time practicing English now, as I did recalling French then, my English would be flawless!

As life grew harsher under the Khmer Rouge and chances of survival dimmer, the strangest, most trivial things popped into my head and took on a bizarre importance. Suddenly I'd think with overwhelming sadness, I'm going to die without ever returning to France or Hong Kong; I'll never again ride in a car or eat in a restaurant, as though these were of vital import. During the day we lived a nightmare, but at night I had wonderful dreams of the places I'd been and things I'd done and seen. The worse my reality, the more delightful were my nightly escapes.

I fantasized about two places in the world that I longed to see before I died. While working day after day in the rice fields, I built a imaginary reality about Tokyo and New York. Then I foolishly mourned my loss of never seeing those exotic cities. These fantasies filled a useful function in the unreality of our everyday existence, but there is a serious flaw in mind travel compared with actually visiting a place. Rather than dispelling myths, I created them. After four years of imagining, no place could be as wonderful as I'd made up my mind New York and the rest of America would be.

As a result, when I landed as a refugee on American soil, I faced the same wrenching confrontation with reality that I had in Hong Kong and France all those years ago. Only this time in reverse. I was shocked to discover America wasn't wall-to-wall skyscrapers, and that people actually had to work for a living.

Well, I've yet to tour Japan, but in my twelve years in America, I've taken the opportunity to fill my memory bank with reality about my new homeland.   Our government may not be perfect but, as a recent American citizen, I can appreciate the contrast between what we have here and what I left behind.

39   A BRIDGE BETWEEN CULTURES
By Dorothea Hubble Bonneau

It was a rainy Sunday afternoon, so my mother and I decided to go to a movie.   I wished my father were home, but he was on his last mission as officer in charge.   He was leading a jump into the Florida swamps where he was a paramedic, training his men for combat in Korea.   They were young men, eighteen or nineteen years old, and they were scared, so he offered to jump first.   There was no wind up where the plane was flying and there was a cloud of fog sitting on the ground not moving.   And so he jumped.   He hadn't counted on the freak wind between the plane and the ground, the wind that carried him to his death.

I was only six when he died; he was twenty-eight.   Sometimes I felt happy my daddy was in heaven.   Other times I got scared and thought they had made a mistake and buried him alive.   Once I tried to dig him out of his grave with a toy shovel.

As I grew older, I began to reflect on the cause of my father's death.   His reserve unit had been called up because of the Korean "conflict."   If there had been no war, my father would have bought that horse ranch we looked at in Colorado.   He would have become a veterinarian.   He would have been able to see his seven grandsons grow up.

Time passed.

I was just twenty when the Vietnam "conflict" began.   All that grief, all that pain came back.   Sometimes I dreamed about little girls whose fathers had been killed; little American girls, little North Vietnamese girls, little South Vietnamese girls. All children of the same God, by whatever name. Sometimes, just as I was going to sleep, I heard the voices of little children calling to me, "Help me! Help me!"

It was when I saw the pictures of the My Lai massacre in *Life Magazine* that I began to pray that I could help in some way to create a kind of understanding between people that would make it clear we are all brothers and sisters of the same God. Brothers and sisters.

But what could I do?

While I prayed the thought came to me. Write. Write about people who have learned how to create peace.

The idea had been planted; I wanted to start, but the time was never quite right. My husband and I had started our family, and I wanted to fulfill my role as mother before I tackled writing seriously.

Following the birth of our seventh son, I returned to teaching. It was then I read Joan Criddle's book *TO DESTROY YOU IS NO LOSS: The Odyssey of a Cambodian Family* to my seventh grade classes. Soon after, Joan spoke at our school, and we learned more about Teeda Mam and her family.

Teeda and her relatives had endured pain, horror, and death of loved ones but, through it all, they kept love and peace in their hearts. They had transcended cruelty and deprivation. Their lives were an example that could give hope to others. It could build a bridge between cultures.

Joan's book had a profound effect on many of my students. Two spoke to me on separate occasions and told me that they had considered suicide, but Teeda's triumph over suicidal thoughts had given them hope and courage. Some students compared the story to *The Diary of Anne Frank*. There are striking parallels, but miraculously, Teeda and most of her family had survived.

This family, whose only revenge was the desire to prove their own worth, had learned to create peace. I felt a strong desire to write a play based on the book. I asked for play rights and Joan agreed.

It took almost two years to complete the play.* When it was finished, I sent a copy to Teeda. Her response gave me chills. I had added the goddess Cambodia to the script; Teeda felt close to this character. "Do you know my name means "attendant of the goddess'?" she asked. Her next question seemed stranger still. "You knew about my friend in the camp," she said, "but nowhere in the book is she named, and I did not tell it to you. How did you know her name was Lon? It is not a common Cambodian name." I couldn't answer.

The next teaching year was remarkable. My sixty, ninth-grade drama students voted unanimously to produce the play. The city of Davis generously awarded us a five hundred dollar grant to defray expenses.

The students and I conferred on all the production elements. One point for consideration was whether to try to make the almost totally Caucasian cast look Cambodian. With Joan's concurrence, we decided not to try. The story is universal; a person of any race should be able to play any part.

In the beginning of the production process, there was tension. Students felt unsure about becoming intimately involved with another culture. "How can I wear a *sampot* on stage in front of my friends?" "I would never agree to marry a man my mother chose for me." Producing a play is different from reading a book. It requires personal commitment and emotional immersion. The distance between cultures melted with time, as did the distance between generations.

After we embarked on the project, Teeda's friends and family helped. I remember the first time Teeda met Casey, who had

---

* *TO DESTROY YOU IS NO LOSS*, the play, published by The Dramatic Publishing Company, Woodstock, Illinois, 1991.

been cast in the lead as Teeda. They looked at each other and began to giggle, then they hugged. "That's good!" Teeda said when she stopped laughing, "A tall, blond Cambodian!" A cousin of Teeda's taught two students classical Cambodian dance. She not only lent us authentic Cambodian costumes, she came an hour before the play to fix the dancers' hair and do their make-up so it was "just right."

During the actual performance there were laughter and tears all around. Teeda's mother, who speaks almost no English, pointed at the stage with delight every time her character appeared. "That's Me! Me!" she said.

Cambodian college students commented that it was a story that needed to be reenacted. One young actress informed me that she taught her entire family about what happened in Cambodia. "My college-age sister didn't even know!"

It is said that once you have seen a white crow with your own eyes, no one can tell you no such creature exists. I believe it is the same with people. Once we have walked in another's shoes, once we have seen how alike are the dreams and feelings we humans hold in our hearts, no one can tell us he is not our brother, she is not our sister.

No one can tell us that to destroy life is no loss. Or that the cost of lasting peace is too great.

40   A MOTHER-IN-LAW

Teeda:

Remember all those jokes you hear about American men and their mothers-in-law? Well Vitou is no different. My mother wants to be in control and is accustomed to getting her way. Vitou is strong-willed too. He is very Americanized, and she is very Cambodian. I'm impressed that they've been able to live under the same roof without too much conflict.

When my mother moved to our home, she assumed she was

in charge, just as she had been while I was growing up in Phnom Penh, when my two married sisters, their husbands and children lived with us. There, Mum ran the household with help from Mearadey, Rasmei, and servants. My dad made the other major decisions and paid all the bills.

Vitou has been an unknown quantity in Mum's life ever since we married. She never raised a son, so he both intrigues and frustrates her. Her four daughters and older sons-in-law view life more as she does. Those sons-in-law are not risk takers, and Mum has always been able to control her daughters, even though we are strong-willed women ourselves. All of us tend to give in to her demands, usually before they become demands.

Vitou is different. He is fiercely independent, probably never will take the cautious route in life, and intends to make decisions in his own home and run his own life. It is little wonder that he and Mum occasionally clash, especially while both were home all day when Vitou worked swing shifts and night shifts.

At one point, there was so much tension that I feared it would not work for Mum to continue living with us. She and Vitou competed over running the household, and when I got home from the office, each vied for my total attention like a couple of kids. Fortunately, things have settled down, especially since Laura and Andy were born. Now we've adjusted to a routine that works well most of the time.

It is customary for Cambodian parents to live with one of their children when they grow old. None of us, including my mother, have ever considered that she'd live on her own - especially not in America. Until Vitou and I bought our house, Mum lived with Mearadey's family. Since we had three bedrooms for the two of us, and my sisters' homes were crowded, Mum joined our household shortly after we settled into our new place.

An early contest of wills between my husband and my mother took place over our home's decor. Vitou and I wanted a tastefully decorated, modern home. Mum thought the glass-fronted china cabinet was just the spot to display her trinkets. Vitou is right in calling them tacky, plastic souvenirs, but I probably would have relented when she got her back up about them staying in the cabinet. Vitou, however, had refrained from confronting her on several other rearrangements she'd made in our home. This time he insisted that her gaudy treasures not be the first thing people saw when they came in the house. After that show-down, Mum flounced into her room where she remained for several hours, her usual response when she is crossed.

Deference to elders is a cardinal principle of Cambodian life, and she felt she'd not been treated with the respect due her. However, there's an equally weighty obligation she'd ignored; since she lived in her son-in-law's home at his expense, she owed him respect.   Her own mother-in-law certainly had not run Mum's household in Phnom Penh. Many times when my mother goes into her room acting hurt, I think it's really because she feels ashamed for needing to be reminded that she overstepped her bounds.

I don't want to give the impression that Vitou isn't patient and gentle with her most of time. He is one of the most patient men I know and puts up with a lot, but he's been the one home with her and the children all day. So he's had to be the one to enforce the rules. He finds that frustrating.

Vitou feels that, although he is thirty-four years old, Mum often treats him like a kid who couldn't possibly know anything. That's probably because she still thinks of me as her "baby girl." Vitou and I are quite a bit younger than my two oldest sisters and their husbands, and Mum has a hard time thinking of us as adults.

Vitou and I love Mum and want her to be healthy and happy. However, she isn't favorably inclined to take our suggestions for maintaining her health, especially when we've tried explaining that her smoking habit aggravates her medical problems. On the other hand, she usually believes what her oldest son-in-law, Ken, tells her. But when he and Mearadey told her about the health risks of smoking, she turned a deaf ear to them too.

Until Laura Tevary and Andrew Tevuth were born, we tried not to bug her too much about her bad habit, but we were not willing to put their health at risk with her second-hand smoke. That resulted in another confrontation between Vitou and Mum. He insisted she restrict her in-house smoking to one cigarette after dinner; otherwise, she must smoke outside. At first, that really made her angry. Because she loves her grandchildren, she refuses to believe that she could possibly cause them health problems by her habits; the logic of modern science will never faze Mum.

Logic of any kind seldom convinces her of something once she makes up her mind. For instance, she became determined that Vitou should put a security screen on our front door and block the nearby window with a wooden insert because she worries about burglars. Vitou pointed out that every window in the house could be broken as easily as the one by the door. If a burglar wanted to get in, one boarded up window would not stop him.

She didn't like that answer, so again Vitou was in the dog house. Fortunately, he's learned to shrug off her bad moods when he can't joke her out of them. An hour or so later, she'll issue forth from her room to watch a favorite television show as though nothing had happened.

I work days, so Vitou continued with swing shift long after he qualified to move to day shift. He'd stayed because he didn't want to burden Mum with the care of our children when they were little. Besides he loves being a father. Vitou is more involved with rearing his kids than any other man I know. After I'd leave for work, he got them up, then fed, bathed, dressed, and played with them all morning, gave them lunch and put them down for naps before going to work. Mum only needed to tend them while they slept. I usually returned from work before they woke. After supper, I played with them until about 10 p.m. when I put them to bed. That still gave me a couple of hours to do housework or other projects before Vitou got home.

When Laura began nursery school and Andy was a toddler, I encouraged Vitou to move to the day shift so we could enjoy a more normal family routine. We hired a woman to come to the house to watch Andrew. My mother has arthritis and is getting old; we didn't want her to be responsible for a preschooler or have to chase after him. We hired a Cambodian woman because we realized it would be awkward for both Mum and the sitter to have another adult in the house if they couldn't communicate. Vitou and I knew one of us would have to set Mum straight before we could bring anyone into the house to work for us. Vitou, dodged that duty, so I was elected.

I said, "Mum, the woman I've hired is not a servant; you must not treat her like one. I know in Cambodia you prided yourself on how good you were to the servants, but that is not good enough here. In America, each person is considered as good as the next. Just because she works for us does not mean you can order her around. We hired her for one thing - to watch Andrew. You must not ask her to clean, cook, run errands, or get you things. She will be totally responsible for Andy. You'll be free to talk on the phone with your friends as long as you want, take a nap, or do whatever you like, but you must not interfere with her work. You must speak respectfully to her, and you must treat her as an equal."

It was not easy for me to be so blunt with Mum. She took it quite well, but I knew it would require more than one reminder to break old habits, even though they had remained dormant ever since we left Phnom Penh almost fifteen years before. It also took the sitter awhile to decide how she should act toward an employer's mother. Ultimately, it worked quite well for both women. They became friends, which eased each one's sense of isolation in a foreign country. That companionship could not have happened if they'd been allowed to fall into old cultural habits.

Although Mum can't adjust as completely to American ways herself, she's proud - if a bit mystified - that the rest of us have. She's impressed that her daughters earn good incomes, even though she has little idea what we do all day. Most of what I do in the computer software industry she could not understand. The rest would only upset her, so I don't mention it. She would be scandalized to know her married daughter occasionally lunches with male colleagues, men who have wives of their own. She'd find it improper that women are sometimes the supervisors of men or that men and women joke back and forth and call each other by first names. If I ever get a phone call at home from a male co-worker, she fears I'm having an affair. In order to meet my husband's and my needs as well as my mother's, I've had to keep my life in compartments more than I like.

I guess it is never easy for three generations to live in the same household or for a mother to trust a daughter and son-in-law to fill the shoes she once filled so capably. In addition, each of us has had to adjust to America at our own speed and find ways to blend our ideas with the ideas of other family members.

When colleagues tell me their in-law problems, it helps me remember that intergenerational conflict is not unique to being Cambodian-American or to being a newcomer to America. It is not just my mother's more traditional, Eastern ways bumping against our more liberal, Western ways. Also, when I see the wrenching family problems many Cambodian-Americans experience, I realize ours have been mild in comparison.

Over time, we've learned we must not try to coerce an outward conformity, or mistake it for genuine unity. Above all, we value each person in our extended family - sometimes despite their individuality! Because we love and respect each other, we've learned to look at the humorous side of earlier confrontations, instead of letting them fester.

I'm especially proud of how graciously Mum has accepted the changing roles she sees her children and grandchildren adopting. As Vitou often reminds me, she's quite a remarkable woman.

41 CHRISTMAS
Interview, Fall 1991

Joan: Christmas was a new tradition. What stands out in your memories of that holiday?

Teeda: The first one and last year. Mearadey, Ken, and their girls had one Christmas before the rest of us got to America, but for most of us, 1980 was our first. I had no idea what to expect.

Rasmei: Mearadey said our sponsors would bring a tree, put a tree in the house! Louise brought a really big one; it touched the ceiling. Members of the your church donated all the ornaments. By the time we'd used all they sent, the tree was full. Imagine how much it would have cost to buy. Instead, we had this wonderful collection from everybody.

Roth: Besides the Christmas balls and other ornaments, we put on aluminum strips called icicles, plus strings of popcorn and decorations we made at school.

Chenda: I remember having my picture taken in front of the tree. I sat by my mom; I think we still have the photo.

Teeda: American friends donated tickets to the *Nutcracker Ballet* in Sacramento. A beautiful theater. A grand production. A really big deal for us. I went in Fowlers' big car.

The part I remember best is the Nutcracker man. There is a similar story in my country about a dancer on the wall who comes to life. A beautiful movie was made of that story just before the Khmer Rouge takeover. The other thing I remember about the night at *The Nutcracker* is the man in the black suit. You call him the conductor? He left the orchestra pit at the end of the performance, went to the stage, and bowed deeply. The people clapped; he came back and bowed again. Then he left and the audience clapped some more. He came back a third time. I whispered to my seat mate, "This guy is so arrogant! Enough of him. Go away!" I didn't know it was the custom.

Tevi: I remember the ballet, too. The elaborate costumes impressed me. I couldn't follow the story, but I liked the performance. At the time, I didn't know *The Nutcracker* was a Christmas tradition.

Roth: I wasn't sure what Christmas was about. I just thought we were going to get some candy and stuff, maybe like I got at Easter and Halloween. At elementary school, we learned a little more about Christmas, what to expect. Santa - a big guy with a white beard who wears red clothes and gives presents.

Tevi: I didn't learn the origin of Santa Claus until high school when a friend told me. But even during our first years in America, I decided he must be a made up character because we didn't have him in Cambodia. I figured that if he really gave presents to all the children in America like they said, he'd give them to Cambodian kids too. Since he didn't come to Cambodia, I didn't believe in him.

Teeda: I didn't know Christmas was a Christian celebration. In my country we had a similar New Year's celebration where people give gifts. Since Christmas was near New Year's, I thought it was part of that. In Cambodia our New Year celebrations revolved entirely around Buddhist customs, so I thought that in a Christian country Christmas was just a New Year's holiday from a Christian point of view.

Sam: It was my family's second Christmas, but I still didn't know what to expect. We kids knew something was up, but we didn't know just what. I didn't realize our sponsors were involved, even though I knew Teeda went shopping with Kathryn several times. Anticipation built. By Christmas Eve, we were really keyed up, still not knowing just what to expect, but knowing it would be special.

Teeda: Several days before Christmas, Kathryn told Mearadey, Rasmei, and me to make a wish list for everyone. The sponsors had collected enough money so each of us could have about $20 or $30 worth of gifts; that's a lot of money for thirteen people. Then she took me shopping for presents for everyone. I got to be her helper.

My family was still having a hard time figuring out why you guys were spending money on our family. You had been helping us ever since we came in March. We were even living in your house while you were in Kuwait. We couldn't help wondering what all you sponsors hoped to get in return; you knew we had nothing.

Rasmei: Since the sponsors were always so generous, Mearadey kept telling Teeda, "Make sure you don't ask for anything too 'spensive. Just get us something little." We didn't want to sound greedy.

Teeda: The stores were decorated beautifully. The things they sold all looked expensive to me. When I saw something unusually nice, I couldn't help exclaiming, "Oh, that's pretty." Then I stopped saying even that, because Kathryn might think I wanted her to buy it for us. I tried to just shut up and not say anything, just walk with her.

Do you know how I got my present? I admired a vest, a knit jacket without sleeves. It was so special that the words slipped out, "Oh, this is beautiful!" It was expensive too - $30, I think. There were lots of colors. She bought it for me right then! I felt so embarrassed; she probably thought I'd been hinting.

That year, the big seller seemed to be Cabbage Patch dolls. People bought them like crazy. I could not understand why anyone would ever want such an ugly doll.

Kathryn kept track of how much we spent, so we'd know how much more to buy for each person. Her priorities were opposite of what I expected. Most of the money went for toys and clothes for the kids. The men got the cheapest presents. We shopped for them last; they got a shirt and necktie.

Ken: That year, our English was almost as new as the shirts. My inability to express myself fluently really frustrated me, particularly on Christmas Eve. Kathryn and her son Bruce brought in all those presents, and we couldn't express how we felt. All we could say was, "Thank you. Thank you." And we kept smiling. We wanted to express more but didn't have enough words to say. We felt embarrassed because we wanted to express more than that, but we just couldn't do it.

Teeda: The day I shopped with Kathryn at Town and Country Village in Sacramento, I got really hungry, but I didn't dare ask her to stop and eat. She is such a strong woman and can go and go. Finally, I saw some bread and cheese samples on a table. I said, "Oh look at that Kathryn," and took a bread cube. She grabbed a piece of bread and cheese. "This is really good cheese, Teeda. Here, try some." I took the piece she handed me, put it in my mouth, and almost died! The cheese was so stinky; it tasted awful. I didn't dare spit it out, so I just bit it in two and swallowed it like medicine. Kathryn kept talking about the delicious cheese; I grabbed a handful of bread and stuffed it in my mouth to take the taste away.

I was afraid to tell her that I thought it tasted awful. It is a terrible cultural habit in Cambodia to deny how you really feel, an Asian trait. One of the things I admire most about Westerners is their honesty and openness about expressing opinions and feelings. This bluntness took some getting used to, however. I have to think about these cultural differences seriously now, because I have two children to raise. I must help them choose the middle ground, avoid the pitfalls in each culture, and take the best from each. They have to learn to balance honesty with not hurting people's feelings. It's hard being raised in one culture and raising children in another.

Tevi: Cultural norms make it almost impossible for Cambodians in America to deal honestly with others in the Cambodian community and in family relationships. The taboos are so strong that you are automatically ostracized if you cross the line. Our family tries to fit in both the Cambodian and the Western communities. It is hard because we have to act two ways. We have to know which behavior to choose in each.

Teeda: Talk about having to choose, when I went Christmas shopping, the stores had too many choices. Kathryn would ask, "What do you think of this?" or "What about that?" I liked everything. I tried to follow Mearadey's instructions and choose practical things like clothes and shoes. It would be special for the kids just to have clothes that weren't secondhand. But Kathryn thought they needed toys also, so each of them got something to wear and a toy or two. She bought Barbie dolls for Chenda Poong and Sam.

Sam: Kathryn knew we wanted Barbie dolls because we played with the other kids in the neighborhood, and they had them. Meg Gabor lived in our cul-de-sac. We liked to play with her Barbie.

Chenda: The dolls got everything - tiny shoes, stockings, combs, everything.

Teeda: We shopped till quite late on Christmas Eve. Our feet ached from all that walking. We shopped in a big mall, F . . . Ff . . . Flo . . . Flor . . . , ya, Fluoride Mall. No, . . . no . . . Florin Mall! Then we came back to Kathryn's. Bruce was home from college or something. He is really tall, a basketball player. He helped bring in the presents. The living room bulged with gifts. Kathryn told Bruce and me to start wrapping while she fixed something to eat. I'd never wrapped a present before, so Bruce showed me how. He took a piece of paper, put the box in the center, measured the paper around the box, and said, "Here, this is how you do it." He put a big flower [bow] on it and everything. I was impressed. Bruce is big like his dad, Del. You wouldn't expect him to do anything delicate because his hands are so big. I kept thinking, this is a big man and he can do so well. He wrapped the beautiful boxes really fast too. And he had fun looking at the toys as we wrapped. He'd say, "Oh, Star Wars! Wow!" "Oh, look at the Barbie!" It was really funny to me because he was a big adult, and he acted like a kid. We filled Kathryn's Honda with gifts, and he helped us take them to our house.

Sam: We weren't sleepy, but we had to go to our rooms when Bruce and Kathryn came.

Mearadey: Teeda came in first. She told the kids to go to the bedrooms, because a surprise was on its way. They were so excited. The adults got to stay in the living room. Bruce and Kathryn brought in so many gifts. We, of course, didn't buy presents for each other, so what they brought *was* Christmas.

Roth: The windows in the hall in the bedroom wing were opaque so you couldn't see out very well, but you could see motion. We could tell they were bringing lots of gifts. We knew it was Kathryn and Bruce. We knew their voices. It took them three or four trips to bring in everything.

Rasmei: As soon as Kathryn and Bruce said, "Goodbye, Merry Christmas," and closed the door, my three kids and Mearadey's three just burst into the living room. They couldn't wait. Tevi and Sam kind of knew about getting presents because they had Christmas the year before; they kind of told my kids.

Teeda: They were so wild. They didn't wait for anything. Everyone grabbed their presents and tore them open. All of us were too excited to wait till morning. They were acting so crazy; I told them to cool it because Kathryn and Bruce were outside watching us. Kathryn had asked if they could hide by the orange tree in the atrium for a few minutes to watch the fun through the big windows.

Tevi: I think that night was like a rampage. Everybody just opened their own presents, not waiting for anyone. Poor Bruce, I bet he got so discouraged at how fast his beautiful wrapping was demolished.

Roth: I'd seen the Star Wars game advertised on television and really wanted it. It was a great gift. I got some clothes too.

Tevi: I got clothes, a bracelet, and a little purse. I'd never had a purse before. It had lip gloss in it - almost like having lipstick. I was in fifth grade then, so it made me feel grown up.

Sam: I got a parka, the Barbie doll, and the doll clothes. But the best part was the ballet shoes. I guess Kathryn knew I wanted to be a dancer like my friend Elizabeth Lowry and like the ballerinas in *The Nutcracker*.

Chenda: Sam and I could hardly believe all the clothes our Barbie dolls got. I was too young to remember much more about Christmas. Chenda Peach and Helena were really little and just got excited because we did.

Ken: That Christmas was a much bigger celebration than we'd expected. Everyone had fun.

Teeda: Joan, remember a few months ago when you asked if we were willing to let you write a book about our adjusting to America? You said we were successful, and you thought our story could help other newcomers not get discouraged and help other Americans understand the problems immigrants and refugees face. Ken looked at you in surprise and asked, "Do you think we are successful?"

I'll never forget your face - you looked shocked that he should question it. You said each person had to decide that for themselves, but you thought we'd done amazingly well. Then you talked about ways of being successful and how different people measure it: money, strong family ties, health, good jobs, being happy, and so on. By most measures you thought we had been very successful. Also, you reminded us that a person is likely to feel more successful at some periods of life than others.

Ken: Well, it was really strange to look at ourselves through your eyes. We had been too busy, just getting by each day, to stop and measure if we were successful. We'd never asked ourselves if we felt successful.

Teeda: Since then, we've thought a lot about what you told Ken. I thought about our first Christmas and compared it with the Christmas we had last year, our eleventh Christmas. We've come a long way in ten and a half years.

The other day, Mum and I watched the video we took last Christmas. This was the first year that Soorsdey, Samol, and Seri could join us. It was really a memorable Christmas. Soorsdey, Mearadey, Rasmei, and I watched a Thai movie with this handsome male singer in it; we let him become our hero for the holidays and made a big deal out of being in love with him. Our children and husbands thought we were crazy. But we even got my nieces to join us in liking him.

Mearadey: He's not really that great, but it was fun to have something in common with these kids. They enjoyed seeing a lighter side to their moms and aunts. One night we all dressed up in our best clothes, had a family portrait taken, then danced and sang and had fun. I think my mother, and especially Ken's mom, thought we had lost our minds. Our husbands tried to ignore us, but we even got them to loosen up in the end. Everyone danced.

Teeda: It was a beautiful family time. My nieces and nephew were more interested in being part of the family again. That hasn't always been true. Lately the older kids aren't denying or rejecting their Cambodian heritage so much.

Rasmei: That's really important to us. I guess they have already done their teenager thing [rebellion] and are turning around. The younger kids aren't at the rebellious, rejecting stage yet. The two Chendas, in the middle, are a little bit over on that side still, but our strong family pulls them back. Even Roth is excited about coming home for Christmas this year. He's at an aeronautical mechanics school in Colorado. It's been kind of hard for Roth, growing up as the only boy with all these sisters and girl cousins.

Teeda: Because I've been thinking about what you said about success, Mum and I watched the Christmas video in that light. I realized it showed us living a good life, a comfortable life. We have all the basics - lots more than just the basics. And occasionally, we can take special trips or enjoy a vacation. Most important, we can get together. Now that my nieces and nephew are pulling for family unity instead of pulling away, it is much easier and more fun. For a few years it seemed like an uneven tug-o-war.

Last Christmas was the first we had wholeheartedly allowed ourselves the freedom of enjoying what we have and our time together.

Ken: 1990 was the first Christmas that my mother was in America. Little Grandma arrived in the country only twenty days before Christmas. She still suffered from jet lag and was confused by all the new experiences. She hadn't seen me for twenty years. Tevi was only four when my mother last saw her; she'd never seen our other two daughters.

Twenty years ago, the Khmer Rouge took control of the area of Cambodia where my mother lived. We couldn't visit her any more, and she couldn't escape. Five years later we were under Khmer Rouge control, too, but still couldn't contact each other. I didn't know if my mother and sister were dead or alive. I worried about them. Because of my education, they were sure I'd been killed, and my family with me.

Mearadey: Looking at ourselves from my mother-in-law's perspective, we realize how much we have changed since coming to America. Our lifestyle is so different; my sisters and I work outside the home. We all rush around and have so much to do. Our children are independent. We are westernized.

Because she is skinny, we call her Little Grandma, and

we've begun calling my mother Big Grandma. Little Grandma came last December and couldn't get warm, not even in the house with a sweater on. So everyone gave her something warm for Christmas. She got fuzzy slippers, mountains of sweaters, sweat shirts, gloves, and hats. She just sat surrounded by that pile looking bewildered but delighted.

Rasmei: We've changed about present-giving too. The first Christmas, it didn't occur to us to give gifts to each other; besides we had no money for non-essentials. Now everyone gives a gift to everyone else. Last Christmas, especially, we went all out because it celebrated ten years in America and the first time we were all together for the holidays.

Teeda: The last year or so has been a turning point in our lives. For most of the past ten years, Soorsdey has felt frustrated and lonely living so far away. It's been hard to be in Canada when she knew we lived near each other. Soorsdey and Samol would like to live nearby, but they've made a good life in Canada. Now Soorsdey feels quite content there.

Rasmei: Their daughter, Seri, got to spend time with cousins near her age - Chenda Peach and Helena. These young teenagers practiced dance routines most of the Christmas holidays and had a great time together.

Teeda: It has been a good time for Ken and Mearadey too. Until recently, Mearadey always focused on making money, money, money. She didn't want to spend any time doing anything else; she didn't feel secure. Now she can take life easier, enjoy trips, and do more things with Ken and their girls. Ken can relax knowing his mother is out of Cambodia where he can take care of her.

Mearadey: Rasmei and Leng's family is closer. At last the kids are past some of the rebellion time, so it is easier for everyone in her family.

Teeda: It's a good time for me too. I relate better to my sisters now I'm a mother. They think of me more as a grown up, not just their baby sister.

Are we successful? After watching that Christmas video, I have to agree with you. This is such a good time in our family.

Rasmei: Gradually we've become comfortable with our lives. Like bamboo in a storm, we were flattened by our experiences in Cambodia and our first years in America. Then we got so busy just living that we'd not really noticed we were upright again.

Teeda: In America it was very hard for a long, long time. Sometimes it seemed impossible that we would ever adjust, that we'd be able to keep the family from fragmenting, that we'd ever get over being poor. Now look how much we spend on unnecessary things for presents!

But family unity is our most valued possession. It is a beautiful gift that we work on very hard.

FREEDOM'S BREEZE
By Helena Hong
7th Grade

Walking through the different air,
    It's as though I'm not really there
Feeling freedom through my finger tips,
    Having the crisp air brush my lips,
Leaving behind Cambodian toil,
    Touching America's fresh soil,
Coming, learning new things,
    Appreciating the pleasure it brings.
Schooling is difficult at times;
    You help me through it, oh family of mine.
All of us successful - jobs, good grades, and more -
    But greater than that, we're together for sure!

APPENDIX I

REFUGEE ORGANIZATIONS

The following list of names and addresses is only a sampling of the many organizations that work on behalf of refugees and immigrants, but it does provide a starting point for those who want to learn more.

International Red Cross
19 Avenue de la Poix
CH -1202
Geneva, Switzerland
phone 22-734-6001

Lutheran Immigration and Refugee Service
390 Park Avenue South
New York, NY 10016-8803
phone 212-532-6350

United Nations High Commission for Refugees
Casa Postale 2500   or   UNHCR Branch Office
CH - 1211   United Nations
Geneva 2 Depot, Switzerland   Grand Central PO Box 20
phone 22-739-8111   New York NY 10017

United States Catholic Conference
Migration and Refugee Services
1312 Massachusetts Avenue N.W.
Washington D.C. 20005

World Conference on Religion and Peace (WCRP)
777 United Nations Plaza
New York NY 10010

REFUGEE AND IMMIGRANT Resource Directory 1990-1991, published by The Denali Press, PO Box 021535, Juneau AK 99802-1535 - compiler, Alan Edward Schorr. This directory, reported to be the most comprehensive in its field in the world, is available at most libraries.

In addition, every state has several organizations to help refugees.

APPENDIX II

What are the major [traditional] value contrasts between Vietnamese, Lao, Khmer, Hmong, Mien, or Chinese cultures and the American culture?

AMERICAN

Negotiable social roles

Look toward the future

Hopeful, optimistic

Success measured in material terms, fulfillment, mastery of challenges

Belief that world operates according to logical laws of science

Status differences minimized, relations informal

Events and relationships organized by time

Discourse style is syllogism: if A and if B, then C

Understanding based on making terms explicit

Interpersonal style . . . confrontation, competition, friendly aggression

Friendships short-term, non-binding

Man can and should conquer nature

Social control based on persuasion, individual appeal, guilt

Individuals possess potential that should be maximized

Children are individuals as are parents;
  to depend on the other is taken as a sign of incompetence

Children are expected to earn their own way,
  not depend on their parents' reputation

From The CHANNEL, a newsletter of the National Association for the Education and Advancement of Cambodian, Laotian and Vietnamese Americans - NAFEA - Spring 1991

ASIAN

Well defined roles, usually in terms of kinship, gender, status

Past generations define and affect present individuals

Accepting, fatalistic

Success measured in terms of accomplishment, correct behavior, status

Spirits, ancestors, past lives cause things to happen

Status differences often codified in the language

Events organized by social relationships

Discourse style is narrative, allegory, parable, proverb, allusion

Understanding requires knowledge of unstated assumptions

Harmonious relations, proper behavior important in social interactions

Friendships long-term, based on reciprocal obligations

Man is part of nature

Social control based on filial piety, propriety, intervention of 3rd party

Good of the group supersedes individual gain

Children owe parents a debt for birth and rearing

Children are an extension of the parents

Used by permission of Judy Lewis, NAFEA

ABOUT THE AUTHOR AND HER WORK

Joan Dewey Criddle, mother of five, grew up in northern Utah and now lives with her husband in California. Her mother claimed that since childhood Joan's motto has been:

Tell me something I've never heard before,
And show me something I've never seen before.

With her children raised, Joan (pronounced JoAn) has turned to writing and lecturing about refugee and minority issues and is currently working on the first-person biography of a Korean-American couple through whose lives this culture's history, customs, and values will be viewed.

The underlying focus of the author's research and writing is to explore how people and cultures adapt to dramatic change; which values and traditions are kept or modified, and which are jettisoned?

BAMBOO AND BUTTERFLIES is the author's second book to focus on the refugee experience through the eyes of one extended family of outstanding Cambodian-Americans. (*TO DESTROY YOU IS NO LOSS* is the first book.) A third book about this family is anticipated - again using the first-person format to further probe family relationships and other issues as the "1.5 Generation" moves into adulthood.

Many in this generation of young Americans - who come to this country as children or are born here to immigrant parents - must make marital, career, educational, and cultural choices unlike those their older relatives faced. How do they blend two vastly different cultures to incorporate the best, not the worst from each? How do successful multigenerational families deal with these differing expectations, values, and goals? How do newcomers cope with prejudice and discrimination? What strengths do immigrants bring to this country, and how do newcomers benefit America and Americans while reaching for their own version of the American Dream? Finding exemplary role models and discovering answers to these and similar questions intrigues the author.

****

INDIVIDUAL SAL̃S and QUANTITY DISCOUNTS